#EVERY BELIEVER

D1519816

BY GREG GERVAIS

Printed in the United States of America
First Printing: June 2022

ISBN-13: 9798835253166

This book may be purchased for educational, business or sales promotional use. Special discounts are available on quantity purchases. For more information, please call or write.

Greg Gervais
8625 Hwy 51, Southaven, MS 38671
www.gregdgervais.com

Book Interior Layout & eBook Conversion by manuscript2ebook.com

PRAISE FOR *#EVERY BELIEVER*

Greg Gervais' new book, *#Every Believer*, is written from the heart of a passionate pastor and communicator of the gospel. It is an easy read that is inspiring and truly encourages one's faith. I believe you will be inspired by *#Every Believer*.

Blessings in and through Him,

Randy Clark
D.D., D.Min., Th.D., M.Div., B.S. Religious Studies
Overseer of the apostolic network of Global Awakening
President of Global Awakening Theological Seminary
amazon.com/author/randyclark
Skype ID randyrayclark

#Every Believer is full of electric testimonies that will stir up within you a fresh passion to manifest the powerful Kingdom of Heaven to the lost through prophetic words, divine healing, deliverance and other signs and wonders. *#Every Believer* will encourage you to lay aside your fear and inhibitions, break unholy apathy within, and embolden you to step out of your comfort zone and step into the Kingdom Zone.

Evangelists Tom & Susie Scarrella

TABLE OF CONTENTS

Foreword 1

Introduction...3

The Sleeping Giant 5

#Every Believer.. 33

The Necessity for the Miraculous 55

Jesus, the Secret Weapon 79

Jesus, the Walking Covenant..107

If Religion Can't Kill Us, It Conforms Us.........................117

Where's the Power?...131

I'm Anointed...151

Practice Makes ~~Perfect~~ Powerful 167

About the Author...203

FOREWORD
THE SLEEPING GIANT

Have you ever felt that there was a giant trapped inside of you, screaming to come out, incarcerated behind self-defeating opinions, excuses and insecurities? If that's you, then perhaps this is more than a book; perhaps it's your key to unlocking that sleeping giant.

I've known Greg for several years now, and I feel somewhat qualified to tell you what qualifies him to write this book. First of all, it would shock those that know Greg now to find out that he, in fact, was Canadian—a culture in itself that comes with various connotations and stereotypes. When God called Greg to the United States, a place he would later meet his wife and come to call home, there was a need for the giant to arise as a man from a country that doesn't reward "giants." Greg has demonstrated over and over again a willingness to move with God in the presence of fear, something that has more than qualified him to write this book. Each page is a journey of his experiences from loss to great triumph, with direction on how you, too, can unlock the sleeping giant. Greg possesses a unique ability to pull courage out of those who suffer the greatest levels of introversion. I've personally watched him mobilize churches to win the lost through radical faith.

Any reader that picks up this book should expect to find a narration by an author with authority to speak into this area. This is not a text book; this is an alarm clock for the sleeping giant inside of you.

Tomi Arayomi

Founder of RIG Nation

INTRODUCTION

Just the fact that you are reading this book proves you are hungry for more than we are seeing in the body of Christ right now. The church is starting to wake up in this hour. I believe there is an "#Every Believer" movement happening, and it is the next "Great Awakening." We are God's empowered agents to awaken the Sleeping Giant in the church and in America.

Join me on this journey and receive the keys that open the supernatural for every believer to heal the sick, cast out demons, make disciples, boldly share the Gospel and win the world for Jesus. The largest move of God and the largest army of love, purity and power is coming together; it is time for us to awaken!

We are equipped by the Word of our Lord and the power of the Holy Spirit to go to war or the war comes to us. What if now is your moment!

God intended for every believer to win this world! There is an army that God is raising up right now and it's you and me! He is pouring out on every believer like never before.

Every believer can hear from God. Every believer can heal the sick. Every believer can cast out demons. Every believer can live a bold life sharing this great Gospel Message. Every believer can be anointed to do what Jesus did and commanded us to do. Every believer can do what Christ did and commissioned us to do upon His leaving. He left us as empowered agents.

God's plan for you was not separate from His supernatural power through you. Your life plus God's power equals the life change of those all around us in this world. It is possible to be powerful. I always meet amazing believers who know God but don't know that they can be used by God in such powerful ways. This book is to awaken the power of God that is for you, for every believer.

I woke up out of a Jesus encounter with an unstoppable urge to do what Jesus did - hear from God, heal the sick, cast out demons, share the Gospel, and more. I had encounters with the Holy Spirit and have seen miracles in so many places since the beginning of that awakening. I realized it wasn't just designed for the pastors or the elect, but for every believer to walk like Jesus walked. This is the message for the Body of Christ, that every believer could represent Jesus everywhere we go - in church, at home, in neighborhoods, marketplaces, business, and all over the world, with power.

God changed me on that one weekend encounter by the power of the Holy Spirit, but even after encounters with prayer, healings, salvations, and success in Jesus kind of living, I was frustrated by a lack of tangible results. This continued for years until I had an awakening 11 years later and had been a senior pastor for two years! Since then, I have seen many healings, deliverances, miracles, and most importantly, believers empowered to walk like Jesus. This book, if you will let it, will impart to you the ability to hear from God, heal the sick, cast out demons, walk in love, and in His power. Every testimony I share and revelation shown just means REPEAT. I'm believing for this and more in you. Join me on this journey to receive keys that open the supernatural for every believer.

1.

THE SLEEPING GIANT

I was coming out of the afternoon session in Dallas, Texas, at the Global Prophetic Summit with Cindy Jacobs, when the Holy Spirit said, "Andrew Wommack is in town." It was a little odd because I was attending a prophetic conference, and I was expecting a word through one of these prophets. I know this is wrong, but I wasn't expecting a visitation from the Holy Spirit Himself. I googled to see if Andrew was in town and sure enough, Andrew Wommack had a conference that weekend, and the last session was in 20 minutes. I immediately drove across town to where the conference was being hosted. As soon as I entered the room, the Holy Spirit visited me, and immediately a vision came to me. Andrew Wommack is amazing, but this wasn't a special Holy Spirit conference nor was there a big movement of people being ministered to; it just happened that God had an encounter waiting for me. Upon sitting down, a vision came to me. It was that of a sleeping giant. The nation I saw was the largest army I had ever seen. Symbolically, it was like the nation of America before it awakened during World War 2. The nation I saw was rich, powerful, and vast in number, yet asleep. Here were millions of souls with a mandate, but fast asleep! The Lord told me the nation I was seeing was the body of Christ. He had deposited so much into so many people but yet they lay asleep.

The Lord then brought into this vision the similarity and significance of the USA during the 2nd World War. If He could awaken them to war, it would be like no other army we have seen yet. It would be another Great Awakening. I believe it's already happening in pockets all around the world, but we need it here, and we need it now! What I'm about to explain is the prophetic state of the body of Christ, and then the mandate that is awakening them one by one.

The body of Christ is so powerful but asleep. Over the years, there have been so many movements, men of God, and reformations deposited into the fabric of the body of Christ. We are on the tipping point of the greatest move of God ever. Although God has poured out so many movements, gifts, and people of God into His body, the things of this world, and all the distractions have diverted the power we were given. We turned to temporary things that we were never called to and perspectives He never gave us. The largest move of God and the largest army is coming together; it's time for us to awaken!

PROPHETIC NATURE OF A SLEEPING GIANT

Since World War I America had been focused on neutrality in certain tensions around the world, including the recently birthed World War II. Even in World War I, America didn't step in until some passenger and merchant ships were targeted by German submarines in 1917. In September of 1939, World War II broke out. Germany invaded Poland but America still remained neutral. Over 90% polled agreed that they should stay out of the war, but if we didn't go to war, war would come to us.[1]

---

1   https://news.gallup.com/vault/265865/gallup-vault-opinion-start-world-war.aspx

"IF WE DON'T GO OUT TO WAR, WAR WILL COME TO US."

America, a country full of wealth, full of fight, full of power, was keeping to itself. It was a peaceful morning on the 7th of December on the Island of OAHU. There were thousands of sailors resting unaware of what was about to happen. Unexpectedly, bomb after bomb began to rain down on Pearl Harbor at 5 minutes to 8:00 in the morning. There were 2,403 lives lost that morning and over a thousand injured. It was said to be a living hell. Nobody could ever foresee an act of war through the Japanese invading America but if we don't go out to war, war will come to us. This one act is what Awakened America to the powerhouse it became. A bully's aggression depends on its victims being passive and not fighting back. In this case, Japan hadn't thought of the vindication it would receive from America, nor did the world think America would rise from its sleep. A great nation, unknown to the world and even to itself, rose to not only fight back against Japan but successfully join allied forces against Germany and win World War II.

THE ALARM IS SOUNDING

The Trumpet is blowing!!! There have been many worldly agendas hit the body of Christ; COVID has come, shootings, racism, riots, and Russia has started to invade Ukraine. What else needs to happen to wake us up? There is a shaking going on!

"Whose voice then shook the earth; but now He has promised, saying, "Yet once more I shake not only the earth, but also heaven." Now this, "Yet once more," indicates the removal of those things that are being shaken, as of things that are made,

that the things which cannot be shaken may remain." Hebrews 12:26-27 NKJV

I truly believe that God is behind the shaking all over the world. Due to a needs-based or humanitarian Gospel, we are praying for things to settle down in the world, but He's shaking it up, and I don't think it's stopping anytime soon. Why? His body is asleep. They have fallen asleep to the cries of comfort rather than to His kingdom. This Gospel has turned into a self-medication or survival message rather than a rescue mission to save this world. People are spending 99% of their waking lives to make it in this world's kingdom and not advancing the Kingdom of Heaven. Jesus has merely become a prayer to pray but not a life to live. Many cry, "pray for this country," or "pray for this city," or "pray for Covid to go away," instead of praying for His kingdom to come and souls to be saved and won. I'm not against humanitarian efforts, but that has become the focus of most believers—although Christ is crying out for His kingdom. The things happening are horrendous, but the hell that is awaiting the world is even worse. Humanitarian efforts are great, but have never been and won't be the focus of the Gospel of Jesus. Yes, God's will is for us to prosper and be in health[2] but that was a promise, not the focus of the New Testament. The hell that seems to be spreading all over the world is nothing compared to the eternal fire, and that can't be prayed away. These shakings are the knockings of the Lord and Savior at the door of the church to return to our first love, which is His Way.

These shakings are a mirror to the awakening of the sleeping Giant of America being awakened when, by bomb after bomb, Japan attacked United States at Pearl Harbor. How many more

2   3 John 2 NKJV

travesties do we need before we arise? I believe this historical account is the prophetic and symbolic time of the body of Christ. As the body of Christ, we have a vast and great company of people all over the world that is waiting to be awakened from their sleep. The problem is, we are asleep! I don't believe we know how powerful we are. I don't believe that most people know how many of us there are. Maybe people were like Elijah who thought he was alone, but there were thousands who were like him, and in our case, there are millions. There are millions of believers who feel powerless and perhaps are waiting on God for rescue, but He has planted in us the power to that is an answer to this cry. Just like with America, they had so much fight, so many people, and more power than they could have ever imagined, and so does the body of Christ. There were enough resources, people, artillery, and courage to win the battle. What America brought to the table tipped the scales to push Germany back. In the same manner, your obedience with God's power equals revival. God's waiting on us to arise.

THERE ARE MORE FOR US THAN AGAINST US

"So he answered, 'Do not fear, for those who are with us are more than those who are with them.' " II Kings 6:16 NKJV

"Yet I have reserved seven thousand in Israel, all whose knees have not bowed to Baal, and every mouth that has not kissed him." I Kings 19:18 NKJV

We have the biggest army in history! We are just sleeping! The enemy is good at tricking people into isolation. Many believers I talk to feel alone about their hunger for more, the ability to hear from God, their belief in the supernatural power of Christ, and their heart to obey Christ, and they definitely don't think there are over 644 million people that are similar. There is an army awaiting to be awakened! This is the 3rd great Awakening! Most believers I run into have a heart to reach the world and represent Christ, but they think that the call is overwhelming or that their part is too miniscule. This heart of defeat has challenged the leadings of the Holy Spirit on the inside. If you could just see that over 644 million believers are in the army of God. That amount of people are waiting to be activated in Christ's power and truly waiting to receive permission to be powerful.[3] Of the 2.38 Billion people who fall under the umbrella of Christ, 644 million people consider themselves to be Spirit-Filled.[4] If you can see that this many believers are alive today, it changes everything. This is our greatest hour!

Have you ever gone to a Christian conference or youth camp? For some reason, being around all these believers, increases your courage and capacity to literally see yourself walking like Christ illustrated before us. What happens when we leave? The sense of support leaves too, but those people are still alive, just geographically separated. The recognition of 7000 prophets encouraged Elijah and seeing how many God has raised up for this era should encourage you. If you could see 644 million people in one place answering the call to bring Jesus to the world in power, it would move you to courageous action. The only difference is that we are geographically separate and the enemy is using

---

3   (https://worldpopulationreview.com/country-rankings/most-christian-countries)

4   In terms of overall numbers, The World Christian Encyclopedia, 3rd edition (2020) currently counts **644 million Pentecostals/Charismatics** worldwide, including all the members of Pentecostalism's 19,300 denominations and fellowships as well as all charismatic Christians whose primary affiliation is with other churches.

that to distract our confidence in Christ, but we are still there in great numbers. There are over 644 million believers who have the power of God, like in the book of Acts, but we are displaced and convinced that we are alone. We are not alone!

If Elijah struggled with this, it's ok that we do. If we can just look at what God's doing and see His numbers, then we will have the courage to arise and demonstrate the Jesus inside and outside of what we call the church. Isn't it crazy that just one shift of perspective could change Gehazi's (the servant of Elisha) mindset? That's all we need, is a mind-shift. As the the body of Christ, we are one nation, under Christ. There have been a lot of bombs going off against us, but there are more for us than against us. What if God is trying to get your attention to rise? What if He's speaking to you to let hope arise again, to read with passion again, to share your faith again, to step out and take risks again? What if now is your moment?

The enemy likes to isolate us so that we change our view of God's story to meet our feelings rather than what God is doing. The devil doesn't want you to be encouraged. He doesn't want you to think there are more for you than against you. Why? Because the day you realize there are more with you, you arise and the Word Himself becomes manifest in and around you—and the devil loses. The Bible says[5] that it was for the Word's sake we are tested. It's not you that's at focus, but Jesus Himself from coming through you that brings attacks against you. If the enemy can get your feelings to cancel out God's calling, then he wins. This is a hard statement to swallow: "It wasn't ever about hurting you; it was about stopping Jesus from walking through

---

5   Mark 4:17

11

you." Let's allow the Lord to redirect our pain toward the true enemy, the devil.

Wow, there is a vast wealth of power just sitting under the rule of neutrality in the body of Christ. Just think, if six hundred and forty four million people awaken to the power that Jesus was talking about, we are in for a Great Awakening. If the one hundred and twenty men in the Upper Room were full of the same power that Jesus had and they turned the world upside down over hundreds of years, imagine what over six hundred and forty four million believers could do? In only months, we could turn the tide of what we've been seeing in the world. Imagine—every believer would hear from God, make disciples, heal the sick, cast out devils, preach the Gospel, move with boldness, and share a love that's out of this world. You personally have what it takes, to turn the tide, but it takes every believer to own His call; it takes risk. It takes everyone of us to get our eyes off this world, and off of what we don't see; it takes opening our eyes to what Christ sees and what He is saying.

GOD IS WITH US

While I was at Fedex, one of my supervisors had been complaining and making mention of severe pain in his intestines. I said to him, "Do you want that to go away?" He just kept talking like he didn't really understand what I was offering. I stopped him, and said, "I mean it, do you want that pain to go?" He said, "Why, what do you got?" I said, "If you let me pray for you, it will be healed." He said, "What?" I said, "Right now, I believe you will feel something leave if you let me pray." He said, "Well, sure." I prayed, "Pain, go in Jesus name, and I thank You God, that Your love is amazing for my friend." I opened my eyes and asked him what was happening. He was like, "No way, it actually went away." I said, "And it won't come back." A few months later he said, "I don't know hardly anyone who I could say is really 'about God' but you, Greg." Now, that wasn't because of me, or because it was only me; I just happened to be obedient and hardly any believers know they can do this.

The name "Immanuel" means, "God with us." *"Behold, the virgin shall be with child, and bear a Son, and they shall call His name Immanuel," which is translated, "God with us." Matthew 1:23 NKJV.* I'm afraid "Immanuel" has been compartmentally romanced into the season of Christmas. Although it's a great time for family, Christmas carols, and a time when more people seem to be nicer, Immanuel wasn't for the Christmas season; it was so we could have confidence because God was in our life here. Jesus brought God into our situations forever. His blood that was shed erased the separation from God that was caused by our sin, forever. He brought God into our lives for good. The Bible says, "once and for all."[6] Jesus paid the price. What does it look like to have God in your life? Jesus. Jesus' life exemplified is what life can look like with God in our lives. Jesus lived a life that we could exemplify. He didn't do any miracles until He was baptized in water and then in the Holy Spirit. He walked as an example of what every believer could follow. The Holy Spirit comes upon every believer to bring God into our stories but mostly to promote Christ's story. God is with us in person through the Life of the Holy Spirit to win this battle for His name. Since He has died for us, all He's asking is for us to live for Him.

---

6   Hebrews 10:10 NKJV

One of the biggest lives that illustrates this "God with us" confidence is David. If you study David's life, he was a man of courage. It wasn't by accident either. In *1 Samuel 16:13 (NKJV)* it says this, *"Then Samuel took the horn of oil and anointed him in the midst of his brothers; and the Spirit of the Lord came upon David from that day forward. So Samuel arose and went to Ramah."* It was the Spirit of God coming upon David that made him mighty. The Holy Spirit Baptism makes us men of war. He gives us a "Can Do" boldness that fills our hearts. A sense of courage approaches us with the baptism of the Holy Spirit. I believe that David killed the lion and bear only after the Holy Spirit came upon him. Even Jesus didn't do ministry or miracles until the Holy Spirit came upon Him. Peter turned from a person who denied Him before servant girls[7] to a person who was historically crucified upside down[8] after the Holy Spirit came upon Him. In Acts 4:31 the Holy Spirit came upon those after they requested more courage or boldness to do more miracles. When the Holy Spirit comes upon us, it brings the confidence that we can do all things through Christ who strengthens us. The Baptism of the Holy Spirit fills our senses that God is with us. What does this mean? It was never based upon our personality but based on His power. Of course we weren't born with the personality to do what Christ asks of us, but that's what His power does; it gives us the ability to do what we couldn't do before.

In 1 Samuel 17 the epic account of David having more courage than all of Israel's soldiers is evident. The children of Israel had walked toward the battle line for 40 days, twice a day, but ran away every one of those times. Goliath was not a typical

---

7   Matthew 26:69-75
8   Acts of Peter 180-190 AD

soldier and not for those with typical training. The crazy thing is, in these last days, typical training is not going to win the war, it has to be our dependence on the Holy Spirit's power that came for the purpose of winning the war. David was anointed by the Holy Spirit to carry out God's purpose in his life. It started with the faithfulness over sheep all the way to conquering the city of Jebus (later called Jerusalem) for His God. Most of the accounts we read of David, and Elijah and almost all who were anointed with the Holy Spirit, we see their confidence unseparated from the circumstance. What? We see that David didn't pray whether it was God's will to defeat Goliath. He knew because of the promise of God and the Holy Spirit on the inside that it was God's will to remove Goliath. Paul healed ALL those who were brought to him on the Island of Malta (Acts 28:9 notes) without a mention of him praying if it's God's will. Jesus didn't pray about the Will of God because God was with Him. Elijah called fire down without the mention of him asking God if it was okay. Peter told Ananias and Sapphira[9] it would be their last breath without a prayer. Am I saying we don't pray about things? No. Am I saying we play God? No, I'm saying we act for Him. One of the biggest misunderstandings (which I will explain later) is with the Holy Spirit. He came for the purpose of making us supernatural. He gives us the confidence that the very things He has asked us to do, He will do once we begin to take the risk. We must be the people and today must be the time!

This world is not my reward; it's my mission. I believe that the biggest problem with the church is a survival or needs based mindset. God is with us, but just like the disciples were living under a false expectation that Christ was primarily there to restore

---

9   Acts 5:1-11 NKJV

the physical country of Israel, many believers are won by a mantra that God wants our physical circumstances worked out perfectly, before we do anything He asked us to do. We've slipped into this needs based, survival first Gospel. I mean, most people, no matter the situation, feel like they are victims of some kind of travesty rather than feel victorious by being found by a Savior. They feel as though God owes them a good life now instead of serving Him first now. If you are born again you have been found by the King of kings, and your goal is not survival now in this world, but the goal is revival. Cute, right? But in all reality, our goal is to represent the true Christ to every single person in this world. The problem is, because of a different vision than the early church, this Gospel isn't preached nor are the supernatural gifts of God exemplified. There has been not just a shift in action but a shift in purpose. We read that faith without works is dead[10], right? The reason why the early church was so different was its vision or its faith. Its faith was not to just survive or prosper in worldly terms but literally to transform the world with the great message of Jesus Christ.

Wherever our faith is, our lives follow. If we believe our calling is to grow families, prosper, and be "ok" in life, then that is where our actions will be. If we truly believe that our life is to make Jesus known to others, we will be about our Father's business. Facts show the state of the church. Ninety-five percent of believers have never led anyone to faith in Christ and 98% don't weekly or regularly share their faith.[11] Is this about evangelism? No, it's about our purpose as the Church. Simon Sinek's book, *Start With Why,* is all about clarifying your why. Our "why" is why

---

10   James 2:14-26
11   https://medium.com/indigitous/train-christians-to-share-their-faith-faa6512f3194

businesses, families, churches, schools, etc. exist. If the purpose of any organization gets watered down or changed, the actions of its employees or representatives change. The church's why, is to disciple the nations. It's the only WHY of the church. If we look at the above statistics, the church has lost it's why. It's not a doctrinal issue so much as it is a missional or loss of vision issue. We've lost who we are.

Even when it comes to Spirit-filled believers, we've lost our mission. The Holy Spirit first came and is still here to make #Every Believer a supernatural witness. His power was to enable an army of love, purity, and power to arise. He came to give us a witness that was out of this world. He didn't come primarily for people to speak in tongues, to create denominations, or just have amazing Sunday services. He came to empower #Every Believer to be Supernatural everywhere. The gifts of the Spirit are supernatural. The Love of Jesus is supernatural. The Purity of Jesus is supernatural. The Boldness of Jesus is supernatural. The Holy Spirit gives supernatural love, purity, healing, freedom, and boldness so we can exemplify these qualities everywhere we go, in order for everyone to know Him. However, here we are using this great power that's been sent from above to just attend church and try to make it through life as we've known it. We are an army, we are co-laborers, sons & daughters of God, and citizens of heaven who have been selected by Heaven and sent on a mission. It is not our job only to survive. This world isn't our reward, just our purpose. Jesus didn't come to save us and then make our lives here on earth full of earthly pleasures, but He came to fill us with a passion that would affect eternity. Literally, our job is to represent heaven, but here we are trying to survive the world just like people in this world. God hasn't called us to be beggars but partners with Him to save the world. It's our opportunity to sit at His table and walk and win with Him. It's our choice to remain survivors or become partners of this great life He's invited us into. We can change the world! What God has given to born again, Spirit-filled believers is enough to shift the tides of evil that are trying to take over this world, and it's enough to reach every person in this world.

THE UNITY OF THE SAINTS

On one of our latest trips to the Philippines and Thailand, we had a average-height 53-year-old white married guy, a 38-year-old African-American single lady, a shorter, 38-year-old single white guy, a tall 55-year-old African-American divorced lady, and me, an ex-Canadian, 37-year-old white married dude. Looking from the outside you may think, *"what the heck do they have in common?"* and maybe, *"boy, that ain't going to turn out well,"* but it was the opposite. We had one of the most powerful times. Somehow, different people with different backgrounds had a peaceful and successful trip. How did that happen? It was unified around the mission. I believe the day we got off our mission and started to be about our versions, is the day we began to be divided.

The unity of the body should be more about our mission than it is the explicit agreement with doctrinal specificities. Just like America awakened and came together, the body of Christ can come together. One person at a time brings multiplication into effect. Don't get me wrong, we don't need to go to the same fellowship, sing the same songs, be the same color, or have the same denomination, we have to just be on the same mission.

God called every believer into the same mission, that is, to win this world until He comes back. Purpose in the community is miraculous. Most believers I meet, although filled with this glorious Holy Spirit, they feel alone. I believe it's because we don't have a common mission or purpose in most ministries. We celebrate and segregate by our differences rather than unify by our calling and purpose as the church. All of those in the military on that day in Pearl Harbor worked together like clockwork. Yes, it was egregious, but together they worked to defend the nation, but most importantly, it was the wake up call that was needed. It's our time to hear the alarm heaven is sounding and come back to war for our Savior.

THE WAKE UP CALL

"WHATEVER WE TOLERATE, BEGINS TO DOMINATE."

The Awakening has begun. Just like America was surprised with Pearl Harbor, COVID 19 hit late 2019 and early 2020 and the church wasn't ready for it. Most of us were lulled to sleep by neutrality. Just like the 90% of America was for neutrality before we were bombed, most of the church is more for neutrality and staying out of trouble with society than they are about winning the war. Most of the church was just trying to survive life as it was, forget an international pandemic. Before war with Russian and Ukraine, COVID, abortion, homosexual and transgender agendas, racism and all sorts of things were hitting the fan—we still didn't wake up. The problem was that every local church and pastor had his or her own mission, and the alarm wasn't sounded for the church to rise; it was sounded for the church to run for safety. This wasn't really about COVID and an international pandemic, but about the church not taking it seriously. Hasn't there been an all-out war against humanity? Against Christ? Aren't we on the tipping point of the world being taken over by Antichrist agendas? Prior to current times, the church has thought neutrality toward all these happenings would keep us safe, but that's why evil is spreading and the church as we know it, is suffering. We can never make peace with the devil. Whatever we tolerate will begin to dominate, and Satan is after our children. The church has responded to the world's pleas to be quiet, as though that was God's plan to win, but it has released even more wickedness in the world. Because we as the church didn't go to war, the war has come to us. So many young people are influenced in schools with ungodly teaching, narratives, and hate toward God. It's time for believers to rise to the occasion, now is that time!

GOLIATH HAS FALLEN

I was in the Philippines and a few of the ministers who had asked us to come over took us to one of the poorer places. They specifically wanted me to pray for this girl with a severe disease. The problem was that her mom and dad were brother and sister and married. Yikes. Incest. What do we do? Was this too big for God? Was this outside the boundaries for healing? No, this is exactly what Christ died for. Paul says it best, *"But **where sin abounded**, grace abounded much more, so that as sin reigned in death, even so." Romans 3:21 NKJV (emphasis mine).* In this situation, I saw this become a reality so powerfully. This girl, who is now a friend on social media, wouldn't even look at me. It seemed as though she was ashamed I was even praying for her. The devil had tormented her with so much shame, but something in me rose up, anger at the devil, compassion from Jesus. I began to pray over and over again, "God, Your love is so amazing for this girl." The presence of Jesus started to pour out. Then I felt this insurgence of vindication against the devil and bound the spirit of infirmity. There was a release in my spirit. I opened my eyes and the girl, who was once bound, looked free. When I started to pray, she was dry, but now she was soaked in sweat. I asked the interpreters what she felt. She looked up at me and smiled this big smile and then gave me a big hug. She said she felt something lift and felt really good. I saw freedom in her eyes. Jesus truly destroys the works of Satan. Sometimes we can put limits or reasons why Jesus can't do certain things, but nothing is impossible to those who believe! [12]

"So it was, when the Philistine arose and came and drew near to meet David, that David hurried and ran toward the army to meet the Philistine. Then David put his hand in his bag and took out a stone; and he slung it and struck the Philistine in his forehead, so that the stone sank into his forehead, and he fell on his face to the earth. So David prevailed over the Philistine with a sling and a stone, and struck the Philistine and killed him. But there was no sword in the hand of David. Therefore David ran and stood over the Philistine, took his sword and drew it out of its sheath and killed him, and cut off his head with it. And when the Philistines saw that their champion was dead, they fled. Now the men of Israel and Judah arose and shouted, and pursued the Philistines as far as the entrance of the valley and to the gates of Ekron. And the wounded of the Philistines fell along the road to Shaaraim, even as far as Gath and Ekron." I Samuel 17:48-52

---

12   Mark 9:23 NKJV

"And Jesus came and spoke to them, saying, 'All authority has been given to Me in heaven and on earth. Go therefore and make disciples of all the nations, baptizing them in the name of the Father and of the Son and of the Holy Spirit.' " Matthew 28:18-19 NKJV

"Inasmuch then as the children have partaken of flesh and blood, He Himself likewise shared in the same, that through death He might destroy him who had the power of death, that is, the devil, and release those who through fear of death were all their lifetime subject to bondage." Hebrews 2:14-15 NKJV

Jesus destroyed the works of the devil. He destroyed them while He lived and He destroyed the power of the devil when He died and rose again. For 40 days, twice a day, the children of Israel ran away in fear from Goliath. It took David to rise up and defeat Goliath for the Children of Israel to have BOLDNESS to go forth and conquer the enemy. This is a symbolism to the death and resurrection of Jesus. When Jesus healed the sick, cast out devils, and preached the Gospel, it destroyed the world of Satan in every person at the same time; it gave His disciples boldness to do the same. When Jesus died and rose again, He told His disciples that He had all authority and power; they were to go and preach the Gospel in this world. In essence, He took care of the Goliath that nobody before Him could, so that His disciples and all of the believers following could do the same. When the Holy Spirit came upon the New Testament church, it was like the light came on, "Goliath has fallen." Go and preach the Gospel, heal the sick, cleanse the lepers, make disciples, cast out demons, etc. was the call upon their lives. Just like in 1 Samuel 17, when all the soldiers pursued the Philistines with courage NOW, instead of fear, the disciples preached the Gospel and moved in power, instead of running away in fear before the cross. The enemy has been defeated. Jesus sends the light into the darkness. But since when was the light afraid of the darkness? No, He has given us His power and authority to carry on His commission until we see Him face to face. It's an act of war to carry out the commission. I truly believe that, prophetically, Goliath has fallen. I don't believe any of these shakings are symbolically Goliath, but the noose of neutrality that has held the body of Christ. The shaking that is happening, including COVID has actually awakened the body to be more alive than ever.

Do you realize that every time you give someone a prophetic word you destroy the works of Satan? Doubt, depression, disappointment, etc. leave when you step out of your comfort boat to encourage someone, whether in church or outside the church. Do you realize that every time you pray for the sick, you destroy the works of Satan in someone's life? Sickness isn't from God now for the most part, so we get to remove it through his name. Every time someone is healed, it is as though a deep wound between that person and God is healed. We should be moving in power on purpose!

Most people who aren't healed have a sense of rejection they feel from God. Like they wonder why they aren't healed. All of a sudden, someone comes up to them and ministers in love and power and that pain in their heart and in their body leaves; it's miraculous. The power of Jesus plays such a crucial role to heal hearts and encourage the reconciliation of so many with Jesus. I find that many are always binding and loosing big spirits in cities and countries rather than just doing what the early disciples did; heal the sick, preach the Gospel, heal the broken hearted, do acts of kindness, etc. I'm not opposed to intercession but if the methods that changed the known world weren't broken, then why fix them? I believe we would see nations turned upside down again, if we would follow the Biblical pattern again. This is true spiritual warfare, but it works!

ESTHER RISING

I remember seeing my wife on the floor passing out. She had an issue growing up and when it was a certain time in the month, pain would fill her body to the place she would lose all consciousness other than her ability to hear. Before we were married I had never seen this in person, but here I was, after our honeymoon, seeing her passing out. The anger and compassion of the Lord filled my heart in that moment for my wife. Yes, as a husband, but this was deeper. It was the Lord Himself filling my heart with indignation He had for the enemy and the love He had for His daughter. I felt authority rise in my heart and stated, "No, this is not going to happen." I began to pray like a man on fire against the works of Satan and a man who dearly loved his wife. I could sense God was fighting through my prayers to deliver my wife from this condition that had plagued her since adolescence. It was a few moments and I sensed the Lord breaking through. As I watched my wife, she began to regain normality and strength. I helped her up and asked how she was doing. It had broken off! Praise Jesus! The good news is God had healed her and it never came back again. There wasn't another pastor to pray; I just had to pray. So many times we are looking for someone else and yet God has positioned us in this lifetime and in this moment for such a time as this.[13] He's looking to enforce His territory through us!

"A copy of the document was to be issued as a decree in every province and published for all people, so that the Jews would be ready on that day to avenge themselves on their enemies." Esther 8:13 NKJV

I believe we are in an Esther 8:13 moment right now. So many believers can see the handwriting on the wall and have secluded themselves in fear but God has called us to fight. Fight for ourselves? No, but for His kingdom. He has given every believer the authority over devils, the power to heal the sick, the Spirit of God to open our ears to hear His voice and prophecy, His love poured out in our hearts,[14] and boldness to say the truth. Mostly, however, we need to take steps of faith to bring Jesus into every situation. In this passage, the Jews had a death warrant, but Esther had a secret weapon, her boldness. Look how this corresponds to this amazing passage, "...by stretching out Your hand to heal, and that signs and wonders may be done through the name of Your holy Servant Jesus... And when they had prayed, the place where they were assembled together was shaken; and they were all filled with the Holy Spirit, and they spoke the word of God with boldness. Now, Lord, look on their threats, and grant to Your servants that with all boldness they may speak Your word..." Acts 4:29-31 NKJV.

Just like they were able to get King Ahasuerus to make another decree so that every Jews could fend for themselves, these disciples prayed to God that they could have more boldness

13   Esther 4:14 NKJV
14   Romans 5:5 NKJV

to preach the Gospel and for more miracles to take place. The mindset of the New Testament wasn't to run or hide, but to ask God for more courage or boldness to do what we are here in this world to do. The boldness of Esther gave her people the ability to free themselves, and the boldness of #Every Believer, bringing Jesus in a powerful way, will bring freedom to nations and make it easier for #Every Believer to really walk like Christ. Then, the end will come. God's not looking for an isolationist version or an evacuation view to save the nations. He's looking for courageous ones, who will believe in the power He has given to them.

It is the believers' job to rid the land of Satan's works. Jesus exemplified what a son of God does. He exemplified what #Every Believer could do, and He showed what God's will was concerning all men. Jesus walked about doing good and healing all who were oppressed by the Devil.[15] The notion that sicknesses, demons, or broken hearts—healed by Jesus, came from God at all would make God to be a multi-personality God. Jesus didn't come to heal people from His Father's sicknesses or issues, He came to destroy the works of Satan.[16] What does that mean? Everything! If you get to know God and His Will, you have confidence to enforce His will on this earth. Just like the new decree gave the Jews boldness to rise up, knowing the will of the Lord will give believers boldness to share this Gospel, heal the sick, cast out demons, and believe in the power God's given them to make disciples. The problem with the church is that religion has brought doubt, confusion, and unbelief.

---

15   Acts 10:38 NKJV
16   1 John 3:8 NKJV

How could David have been bold? He knew he was anointed, and He knew God's will for Israel and the land that had been promised to them. Faith comes by hearing the revelation of God's Word or His voice.[17] He knew the boundaries that were promised to God's people. Many things in the Old Testament are a mirror or an example to us about our life with Christ.[18] God was explicitly clear when it came to the directions about the promised land. He said, *"However, in the cities of the nations the LORD your God is giving you as an inheritance, **do not leave alive anything that breathes. Completely destroy them."** Deuteronomy 20:16.* When God reveals His Will and purposes, it gives us confidence to enforce them. The more we truly know Him, the more strength we get to enforce His Will. The Bible says, *"'Those who do wickedly against the covenant he shall corrupt with flattery; but the people who know their God shall be strong, and carry out great exploits." Daniel 11:32 (NKJV).* It didn't say the more we know Him the more religious we get; the more excuses we have for Him not showing up, the more neutral we get; it said we will be strong and carry out great exploits. Knowing the will of God gives us the confidence to remove the enemy. It gives us confidence to do the works Jesus did, not come up with justifications why they aren't happening. If you don't know what the will of God is or what is from the devil or what's from God, you will never have the passion or faith to remove the enemy from the land. How did all those who became great become great? By believing God's revealed will. By believing God's side of the story. Hebrews 11 isn't a chapter about God's sovereign choosings, but man's responses to God's revelation of who He was or His

---

17   Romans 10:17 NKJV
18   Romans 15:4; 1 Corinthians 10:11 NKJV

will in a situation. We have a choice to believe God's revealed Will or believe our own side of the story, which is usually pain.

I want you to look at the difference between David and Saul. They both had the same word, the same anointing, and the same possibility to accept rejection instead of God's acceptance. Saul looked at himself from the least of all tribes, the tribe of Benjamin, and his family the least of all families in that tribe.[19] David wasn't even considered by his dad to be at the anointing service for the next king. Imagine, the Scripture[20] about not looking on the outside was made by God for you, so that the prophet wouldn't pick a more typically qualified man. David had a chance to take this as rejection. There will always be an opportunity to take rejection from man over the love and affection of the Father. David chose to believe God's report over his earthly father's, and maybe even the prophet's choosing. We all have this opportunity. Pain comes knocking, and I know—it's real. It's so close to home. All the people who should have been there weren't, and bad people who shouldn't have been there were there. The devil wounds us when we are young, because he statistically knows that most will take the pain side of our stories instead of God's invitation and revelation side of the story. But that changes today! You will go free. You will accept God's side of the story. Even now, stop reading, ask God if there is an area the enemy is using to keep you in your story rather than believing His side of the story. I promise, pain will happen if you live in fear, or if you rise in faith. Fear promises us protection but it doesn't pay. Faith and perseverance equals pay off. Okay—let's fast forward to Saul's end and David's end.

19 1 Samuel 9:21 NKJV
20 1 Samuel 16:7 NKJV

The prophet visits Saul in 1 Samuel 15 to deliver news that Saul's reign is over. God was done with his disobedience. Why do I bring this up? Remember at the beginning of Saul being anointed, Saul responded with insecurity? He never let it go. If we don't let go of our side of the stories, it will become a prophecy for our lives. Samuel delivers the message to Saul and Saul apologizes, but asks Samuel to come and worship God and pardon his sin. Samuel says no and turns to leave. Then Saul grabs his garment and pleads for Samuel to return, so he can be honored in front of people.[21] He let the rejection of people kill him and, even when God was done with him, he just wanted the acceptance of people over God. Insecurity doesn't go with time; it goes with trust. The Bible says[22] that David fulfilled all in his generation. What was the difference? David took God's side of the story. Yes, David sinned, but he didn't make excuses for his sin; he repented. He always took God's side of the story to strengthen himself on the inside. What is the moral of this story? That the right version of God's story for you will activate a faith toward God, love for His people, and an indignant outlook against the works of Satan. The Word of the Lord always equips us for war. The revelation of the Lord always produces faith in our hearts.[23]

Secondly, when we don't remove the enemy, the enemy moves into our territories. The devil isn't about to just give up your nation without a fight nor does our neutrality convince him to leave. The Bible says to resist the Devil[24] and he will flee. That resistance wasn't a static resistance but an active resistance.

---

21 1 Samuel 15:30 NKJV
22 Acts 13:36 NKJV
23 Romans 10:17 NKJV
24 James 4:7 NKJV

The Bible says that the gates of hell will not prevail against us.[25] Gates are not chasing us but keeping us out. If we, as the body of Christ, aren't actively or forcefully moving forward, there is no resistance to the enemy, but just opportunity.

ENFORCEMENT

If you look at Israel with the promised land, God was with Israel, but it was Israel's job to keep pressing in to remove all the enemies. I stated before, "whatever we tolerate begins to dominate." God warned the Israelites if they didn't remove the inhabitants of the land, they would become like thorns in their side. In Judges 1 we read that they didn't cast out all the enemy, and in Judges 2 how not persevering to remove the enemy was their responsibility. Wait a second—it's up to God, right? No, it was God's power that was with Israel and His revealed plan that was given to them. God always works with people. It's tough, I get it. I'm sure they had worked hard to remove some of the enemies but for the angel of the Lord to be sent with correction, maybe they gave in to the constant threat of battle. The problem with giving in is, it doesn't help. It just makes things worse.

"But if you do not drive out the inhabitants of the land from before you, then it shall be that those whom you let remain shall be irritants in your eyes and thorns in your sides, and they shall harass you in the land where you dwell." Numbers 33:55

"And you shall make no covenant with the inhabitants of this land; you shall tear down their altars." "But you have not obeyed My voice. Why have you done this? Therefore I also said, 'I will not drive them out before you; but they shall be thorns in your

---

25 Matthew 16:19 NKJV

side, and their gods shall be a snare to you.' " "So it was, when the Angel of the Lord spoke these words to all the children of Israel, that the people lifted up their voices and wept." Judges 2:2-4

Just like God gave the children of Israel the promise and command for the promised land, God has given us a mandate to follow His Word. Remember, this world wasn't our reward nor our protection, it is our mission field as believers. Jesus, who was God in the flesh, told us to make disciples of all nations, teaching them to observe everything He had told the disciples.[26] In today's day, possessing the promised land or removing the enemy looks like healing the sick, loving our enemies, casting out demons, giving a word to the weary, making disciples, sharing the Gospel, doing acts of kindness, and more. It's simply following the pattern, not of this world or anybody else, but the pattern Jesus exemplified. It won the war with the New Testament church and it will win the war here still. Why change what is working?

Israel could have been waiting on God to remove all their enemies but God told them to remove them. The body of Christ has been asking God to do what God has asked us to do. As believers, it is time to get trained again in the works of our Lord. He wasn't just a one time show to wow the masses, but a pattern of living that would turn this world upside down. It's our job to rise again!

---

26 Matthew 28:18-20 NKJV

2.

#EVERY BELIEVER

We were in Thailand teaching at the Bible College on this very subject. My goal is to see them doing this on their own, without me, but I only had 5 days. We were having great sessions; the Holy Spirit was there, super powerful. By the 4th day, it was going "good," but they were still not getting it. On the fifth day, after we went out with them to illustrate how to approach people, we felt a breakthrough. So I started to look for evidence for what we felt. My team and I were relaxing in the courtyard and, out of nowhere, the students came up from behind us with some apparent excitement. They couldn't wait to tell us of healings they had seen and words they had received while they were out. I said, "You guys went out?" They said "Yes! We wanted to try this out on our own, and it worked." Wow! This is the true role of the five-fold minister—to empower those who are willing to move like Jesus!

PERMISSION GRANTED

I woke up with an undeniable urge to preach the Gospel, heal the sick, and cast out demons. Although I grew up in a church that was Spirit-filled, there was hardly anyone who shared their faith, other than the street's mission directors. I had received power and authority to go. It was a new day! Something had changed. This timid man was changed into a passionate representative of Jesus by the Holy Spirit. The good news was that I didn't believe I had been inundated with religious ways to stop what God wanted to do. My first witness wasn't tongues, but power! Then came the dreams and visions the next week, followed by a passion and boldness to prayer walk and share my faith. As I saw sick people, it was like the Holy Spirit had me pray for them. A new me had happened! It was like He had sent me! Just as Samuel said the Holy Spirit would change Saul into another man,[27] my personality was changed by His power inside of me.

You have permission to be powerful! The Holy Spirit came to give you power. He came to ordain you for His use. He didn't come upon you to mainly give you a denomination, a neat experience, or the gift of the Spirit. He came to give you power to be like Him everywhere you go. Do you realize that the baptism of the Holy Spirit came to set us free from ourselves? It's not just a cool experience to align with a denominational belief system—not just tongues, but power! Yes, you were equipped and infilled with the authority and power to operate in the resurrection power of the Holy Spirit, if you have been baptized in the Holy Spirit. I will get into the breakdown of this later. Just as Jesus was to the disciples, so is the Holy Spirit to us. He equips us and sends us by His power. Look at the disciples when the Holy Spirit came; they didn't sit or sign up for more teaching, they went! I'm not opposed to teaching, but I believe this generation has more access to knowledge than Paul the apostle did. It's time to be free!

27 1 Samuel 10:6 NKJV

We have learned to serve and not to slay. We have learned how to be lambs instead of lions. For some reason, we sit and serve the men and women of God and think that was the commission. We've even trained people professionally to serve. Now, that's not bad, but that wasn't the thrust of the New Testament. The Holy Spirit came to make #Every Believer powerful as well as humble. That's why our Covenant is so powerful. We have a personal Savior and personal power for #Every Believer. Yes, it's great to be submitted to a person for growth and relationship, but not just to sit. I believe God is awakening a vast company of believers to see the power that has been deposited inside of them. That's the power to slay! Heal the sick, cast out devils, hear from God, make disciples, and change the nations. So we need to respond to this grace!

It's almost like people are waiting for God to do what He's called us to do. Are we waiting for another lesson, another conference, another pastor to preach and lay their hands upon us? I believe we are waiting for this right here, to be awakened. When you were baptized in the Holy Spirit it was like the time Jesus appointed His disciples. He gave them power[28] to represent Him by healing the sick, casting out demons, and preaching the Kingdom of God. The Spirit of God is a person and He has some to send us. He didn't come to just be with us or to join church services, He came to set us free from ourselves and then commission us to preach the Gospel. So many still feel ill equipped to do things for Christ. I do believe in learning, growing, and being discipled, but not just sitting. I truly believe this is why many men don't like church. We were born to slay.

---

28 Matthew 10:1 NKJV

The anointing that comes on you is just as powerful as the anointing that came on the Old Testament prophets and kings. In Joel 2:28-32 (NKJV) it says, *"And it shall come to pass afterward that I will pour out My Spirit on all flesh; Your sons and your daughters shall prophesy, Your old men shall dream dreams, Your young men shall see visions. And also on My menservants and on My maidservants I will pour out My Spirit in those days."* The Bible is saying that everyone is going to hear from God now. It wasn't just going to be some prophets or some big men of God, but the New Covenant was going to be much more powerful,[29] because #Every Believer was going to be anointed. We were all meant to be sent. It meant that everyone of us was going to be powerful. It took the limits off of us and set us free. It's no longer a few of us that are powerful; it's transforming everyone to be powerful. That's the danger with religion, it makes the power of God of no effect.[30] Religion has duped us into a less than Mosaic covenant. We just attend church, but still have no power. That's why 1 Corinthians chapters 12 and 14 were written. They were written to bring clarity into this amazing power that had been pouring out. Why did Paul say to only have 2 or 3 prophesy?[31] Because it was breaking out too much, and people were prophesying all over the place. Healings and different gifts were operating almost to the place of chaos. Paul was finding it necessary to correct them. Everyone seemed to be anointed. I yearn for this day again. What a good problem to have! Now, there seems to be an opposite problem. Nobody seems to hear from God, nobody heals the sick, nobody has a tongue with an interpretation, etc. But it's going to change. I'm not for chaos or

---

29 2 Corinthians 3:8-9 NKJV
30 Mark 7:13 NKJV
31 1 Corinthians 14:29 NKJV

against order, but I'm against religion and the lack of power in the church! You have permission to be powerful.

The Holy Spirit came with purpose in mind. In Luke 4:18 Jesus quoted Isaiah 61. He said the Spirit of the Lord was upon Him to do some things, not just a denominational thing. It came to send Him. The Spirit is on you to send you, He came to make you powerful. We are sent ones. The Holy Spirit comes as God's hand upon every believer so they will have confidence they are backed by heaven. We are always looking for permission to be powerful, as if a man has to say it's ok to operate in the power of the Holy Spirit. I am not talking about being without accountability or being a maverick, but I am talking about having permission to be powerful. It's fine if pastors don't want you to operate in the church, there are over 7 billion people outside of the church. Nobody is really limiting us. That old Elijah-Elisha teaching has put dreams in the grave. People really believe they have to serve to get power. Yes, don't get me wrong, leadership has to be proven and we don't set anyone in leadership too soon,[32] but we need to start using someone and getting them activated in the Holy Spirit immediately. Jesus gave His disciples power right away. The faithfulness part wasn't so much about earning a place but developing a certain Way. It was an adoption of those disciples while He showed them how to operate.

This is why Ephesians 4:11-12 was written: *"And He Himself gave some to be apostles, some prophets, some evangelists, and some pastors and teachers, for the equipping of the saints for the work of ministry, for the edifying of the body of Christ."* It was to equip or empower #Every Believer to do the work of

32 1 Timothy 5:22 NKJV

37

Christ, not just the janitorial duties. Look, if people don't want to serve and do menial things, it shows the heart anyway, but there is no excuse not to teach all believers to do the works of Jesus. It's just like anything else; there will be chaff and wheat. We just train the same, and time will tell who is a true son or daughter in the faith. The Holy Spirit power also gives humility! So eventually we will see. Jesus came to empower every believer with His power through the Holy Spirit in order that the whole world could see He is the Way. It was the last pull to win the world.

Evangelism is scary. Right? Somehow people paint this word evangelism with a horror paint brush. It's only hard because it's been without power. The expression of Jesus comes with the baptism of the Holy Spirit. What a joy it is to invite someone into the kingdom! What an amazing experience to relate to someone that Christ loves them, and they experience His power because of it! Many have had words of knowledge, healings, prophecy, or just a tangible display of His power to prove His love for them. It's the most marvelous thing to see Christ come on someone. Evangelism is nothing other than disrupting someones bondage to the devil to show them the freedom of Christ. This Gospel is so full of power. The Holy Spirit teaches you as you go and speaks to you almost every time you reach out. It's His plan. He's made you powerful to pray for someone, to heal, to prophesy, to deliver, or to bless them with a coffee. It's the Kingdom of heaven and you and I get to participate.

MULTIPLICATION

There is power in numbers! Addition is great but multiplication is Jesus. The age old Scripture says it all, «*How could one chase a thousand, And two put ten thousand to flight, Unless their Rock had sold them, And the Lord had surrendered them?"* Deuteronomy 32:30 (NKJV). Now, contrary to popular confession, it meant how the enemies would become a curse to God's people when they disobeyed God, but the PRINCIPLE still is alive. The more that join together, the more the influence to convince people of the Holy Spirit's legitimacy. Critical mass, according to *Merriam Webster*, is described as "a size, number, or amount large enough to produce a particular result." As a certain belief system or movement of actions is consistently applied, its effect changes the culture it erupts in. Jesus, His love and power, was never to be kept to just a few people, but multiplied in and through #Every Believer. This is what the New Testament Church did. We overtake the world when we multiply.

It is even in our DNA as humans to multiply, to reproduce. It wasn't ever meant for only one of us to do the work—to lead, to preach, to live the life Jesus was sent to exemplify.

"Then God blessed them, and God said to them, 'Be fruitful and multiply; fill the earth and subdue it; have dominion over the fish of the sea, over the birds of the air, and over every living thing that moves on the earth.' " Genesis 1:28

The good news is, it's in our DNA to reproduce what God's given us. All over the world, even ungodly or secular organizations or religions try to reproduce. Multiplication is a universal law and blessing from the Lord. In the beginning, He told Adam to multiply and have dominion over the land in the garden of Eden.[33] That blessing or empowered right of humans is still working. Look at McDonald's; they made a working model and

---

33 Genesis 1:28 NKJV

then sent it to the world. There are over 37,000 McDonald's in over 120 countries. Look at the false religions. They are more convinced to replicate than we are. They are not contaminated by a limited view, because they understand the principle. When we understand the why, we begin to comply. If our goal is "us four and no more," and to be individualistic or independent as people, then multiplication doesn't matter. But if the goal is to impact the world, then multiplication is everything.

MULTIPLICATION IS SIMPLY DISCIPLESHIP

It is a Biblical foundation. The commission was to ensure replication, in order that the same Way would continue until Jesus comes back. Replication was to secure geographical influence. Influence was to change culture, and culture once established, is king. Discipleship is a foundational principle and imperative practice in the Bible and in early church. It is what kept the working model of Jesus Himself in a pure form.

Gold loses its value once you start adding other metals or materials into the mix. It isn't as valued once the mixture is incorporated. Pure gold definitely costs more than many can afford to buy, or in this case, follow, but it is always admired from afar. Power and purity costs everything because it is priceless. We have watered down the version Jesus intended to appease everyone's own comfort levels. The training Jesus illustrated was always to be followed and reinforced as we discipled people. Too many want to be their own thing but that is what has made the body of Christ stagnant. This world, or the enjoyment of it, is not our reward. Let's buy that gold, refined by the fire of obedience for it is strength for the body of Christ.

The strongest armies of this world are not the least trained or the most opinionated. It is hard, yes, but just because it's hard, we cannot change how the armies of heaven operate. The military is hard, but the military wasn't intended to serve the needs of those serving, but to use those who had given their lives to the military. The training of the military is repetitious, corporate in practice, and personally expected. Why? To make the lives of those in the military hard? To not identify the unique personality of every individual soldier? No, it's to ensure we win the war and protect the territory we have already obtained in earlier ages. There is a saying that sums it up: "*Whatever we tolerate begins to dominate.*" We reach people with love but we are motivated by wisdom. Although the love of Jesus compels us to reach people, the wisdom of the Lord must partner with that love to see the necessity of the mobilization, so we reach every believer's potential.

"WHATEVER WE TOLERATE BEGINS TO DOMINATE."

A pastor friend had organized an outreach to serve an area in Whitehaven in Memphis. I asked him if I could pray for people who came. He was happy to let me. I started asking people if they had pain and prayed accordingly. They were getting healed all over the place. Lines started to form as I ministered to those in this outreach. I know now why Jesus said to preach the Gospel to the poor; it's because they are more desperate. Most of those who had come for free food, clothing, and some community services were grateful for things they couldn't afford. I had to leave, but there were still people waiting for prayer. As I left, a guy asked me to pray for his leg, and he was healed. Then I said, "You pray for the people that are still waiting; I have to go."

Walking out, a young guy named Branden opened his car door and asked, "How do you do that?" I said, "Do what?" He said, "Heal the sick." I simply said, "Do you have any pain in your body?" He answered, "My knee and wrist." I prayed for both, and he said all the pain was gone. His friend jumped out of the car and said, "My back hurts, pray for me." I sensed it was a spirit of infirmity and rebuked it. I felt something lift, and I asked him, "What do you feel?" He answered, "The pain is gone—oh my gosh." Then again, Branden asked for me to train him, so I told him where to find me. Well, about 3 months later, he found me at my church and asked again for me to train him in healing. I agreed. I spent about 4 hours straight going through some of the training we have, and it seemed to break through with his under-standing. I kept in contact with him and people all around started to get healed. He was hooked. I eventually heard this testimony from him. A lady at his job had stage 4 cancer. She was not giv-en hope by her doctor for any chance to live. Her husband was an atheist and had refused to believe in Jesus. He said, "I won't believe it unless she's healed." This was the backstory that Bran-den didn't know before he was about to pray for this lady. He cursed the spirit of death and commanded the infirmity to leave and believed for healing to erupt in her body. Healed! She came back with the doctor's reports later saying the cancer had gone into remission on its own, and she was going to live. Wow, then her husband gave his life to Christ as well. What just happened? Two things. Multiplication of revelations that the Holy Spirit had shown me and mobilization of the power Branden already had. Most Spirit-filled believers don't understand that the power of the Holy Spirit, if they have been baptized in the Holy Spirit, literally came to give witness through power in circumstances just like this. Most people need an awakening to what's already inside and training to change their minds, so God's power can easily work through them. Consequently, we have trained many people who see God's hand move mightily but Branden had so much hunger to see this, I haven't seen too many people rise to his level.

You're next in line. This only came about by renewing his mind and a few hours of training with Branden. Most of that training is in this book. It's really recognizing what's already in you and the secret weapon we already have. You have the power! If you've been baptized in the Holy Spirit, it's in you! The Holy Spirit came upon you to send you. You have permission to be powerful and permission to be used by God everywhere you go. I'm not saying to take over your church, but to take over your jobs, cities, neighborhoods, and more **for** the kingdom of God. It is in the power and the power is in you already!

THE START OF FREEDOM FOR #EVERY BELIEVER

The basis for every believer is believing that God's intention through the life, death, and resurrection of His Son, through His Holy Spirit's power, would give them a personal connection with God. Believing would also open their spiritual ears to hear His voice, open their Spiritual eyes to see visions, and give them a heart that could understand.[34] One of the biggest reformists is Martin Luther. He really came to the surface around 1517. One of Martin Luther's main arguments was the legitimation of every believer as their own priest. He wrote:

---

34   1 Corinthians 2:9-10

"That the pope or bishop anoints, makes tonsures, or-dains, consecrates, or dresses differently from the laity, may make a hypocrite or an idolatrous oil-painted icon, but it in no way makes a Christian or spiritual human be-ing. In fact, we are all consecrated priests through Bap-tism, as St. Peter in 1 Peter 2:9 says, 'You are a royal priesthood and a priestly kingdom,' and Revelation 5:10, 'Through your blood you have made us into priests and kings.'»[35]

For far too long apostles, prophets, evangelists, pastors, and teachers have been known for being worshiped or commanding servanthood, rather than by making believers powerful. Don't get me wrong, I'm not for mavericks and people who talk bad about the church. I don't support those who think their pastors are limiting them. They may be, but there are over 7 billion peo-ple we can reach. My job is to build people, not build my ministry. The biggest blessing to me is seeing people pop like popcorn. I look forward to seeing the body get this for themselves. I be-lieve that's the heart that everyone in leadership needs to have.

*"He who descended is Himself also He who ascended far above all the heavens, so that He might fill all things. And He gave some as apostles, some as prophets, some as evange-lists, some as pastors and teachers, for **the equipping of the saints for the work of ministry, for the building up of the body of Christ**; until we all attain to the unity of the faith, and of the knowledge of the Son of God, to a mature man, to the measure*

35 Martin Luther, *Weimar Ausgabe*, vol. 6, p. 407, lines 19–25 as quoted in Timothy Wengert, "The Priesthood of All Believers and Other Pious Myths," page 12 "Archived copy". Archived from the original on 2015-10-11

of the stature which belongs to the fullness of Christ." - Ephesians 4:12,13 (emphasis mine)

Even the Baptism of the Holy Spirit was to be poured out on "ALL flesh" in Acts 2:17. It was a fulfilled prophecy from Joel 2:28-30. God's plan was to empower His army with His power. If His power was to make EVERY BELIEVER as powerful just some of the prophets of the Old Testament, we can change the world. The Holy Spirit's power was designed to make every person really be changed, have the Word come alive to them, and fill them with a desire to see everyone come to know Jesus Christ.

I'm a senior pastor. Many people think that what I'm about to go over makes people mavericks, can't work, doesn't help the church or won't work for everyone, but I believe by the end of this book you will believe the opposite. We are called to empower every believer to do the works of Christ (the ministry) in order that THE CHURCH can mature and that the world can see Jesus in real time. Jesus was into discipleship more than just attendance, and they weren't the same thing. I am totally for spiritual authority, not spiritual control. We don't need permission to heal the sick, prophesy, or move in miracles outside the church. The Bible does say not to lay hands on anyone suddenly (1 Tim 5:22) for leadership in the church. For whatever purpose, I don't support inviting people from a church you went to in order to build your own discipleship group or house church. I totally support every believer being able to run discipleship groups that consist of converts they have won themselves and disciple them regularly themselves. I am clarifying so people don't go maverick on me and use me for a vice to cause division in a church. I realize pastors may be religious, but again, there are 7 billion people to work with, not other pastors' flock. Leave in peace.

LIONS NOT LAMBS

God's intent was that #Every Believer would be the answer for the world. Instead, we have a bunch of believers who have been taught to sit and serve instead of slaying like Christ exemplified. All throughout the body of Christ we have people who have been trained to submit, trained to serve, trained to attend, etc. but not trained to kill. What? We have equipped people for the system of the church and not for the walk of Christ. I love what my wife says, "We've trained people to be lambs instead of lions." Yes, they should serve, yes they should have a humble submitted heart, but for what? For a man of God to slay? Yes, serving is good and has its place on Sundays, but we've made it people's purpose. David didn't let serving replace his slaying. He served but had a heart to slay. I believe that the church has replaced slaying with serving. God has designed #Every Believer to destroy the works of the devil like Christ did. What does that look like? Not being tame! When the Holy Spirit came upon you, a fire was lit on the inside. The only thing that stops that is the culture of compliance. Most of the body of Christ would prefer us to be compliant to the system of the church we've built. Don't get me wrong, it does some good, but it doesn't equip believers with the power and passion of the Holy Spirit to bring Jesus everywhere.

"WE HAVE TAUGHT PEOPLE TO ROAR PROPHETICALLY INSTEAD OF ROARING PERSONALLY."

Look at 1 Samuel 17 vs 26 as David goes up to the men and says, *"What shall be done for the man who kills this Philistine and removes this disgrace from Israel? Who is this uncircumcised*

Philistine that he should defy the armies of the living God," and his brother corrects him for doing so. He corrects him for not being compliant to the code of people who don't slay. They taught people how to show up to battle but not to win. They taught them how to roar prophetically but not personally. They would all line up corporately but nobody had the faith personally. That's just like today's church; we show up corporately but not personally. For example, we say, "My church serves the community," "Our Church is prophetic," "Our Church does evangelism." I've seen prophetic services which were so awesome. They were telling everyone to roar together, but didn't empower anyone individually to roar after they left the meeting. We don't teach people to prophesy personally, heal personally, deliver personally, evangelize personally, disciple personally, or roar personally. God is raising a lion like roar in #Every Believer to be able to roar on their own. There are those who actually get upset at people who start to heal outside the church, and prophesy outside or inside the church. They get upset with those who take down the Goliaths that the church has been yelling at and then running away from for decades. It's time for us to roar!

When Jesus came, He roared. He was called the *"Lion of the tribe of Judah."*[36] He brought the fight back into believers. He flipped tables, destroyed the works of Satan, and suffered purposely through the cross for us. He was the Lamb for our sins but a Lion inside. He demystified God, His Will, and His Way towards man. Instead of a few, seemingly esoteric individuals, He was giving power to #Every Believer. He distributed His power to every believer. It was His power poured out onto every person that would save the world. Religion always wants to worship

36 Revelation 5:5 NKJV

leaders, limit its people, over complicate being used by God, and relics the movement of God. It is built out of insecurity and thrives on the worship of man.

If you read the following Scriptures, the anthem of the New Testament, and the heart in the Old Testament, it was for every believer to have a personal relationship with the Lord and for every believer to be used powerfully by Jesus in everyday life. People will read this or hear me and say, "What am I supposed to do, quit my job and do this full-time?" It's not an either or; it's just a heart change that says, "Yes God, use me." This book isn't for those who don't want to be used by God or those who just want to be skeptical again or another book that proposes God's power for every believer. This book is for those who know this is possible, who are looking for permission to own this mandate on your life, and for the most part, I believe that's you, the reader.

MOSES, YOU GO TO THE MOUNTAIN

Then they said to Moses, "You speak with us, and we will hear; but let not God speak with us, lest we die." And Moses said to the people, "Do not fear; for God has come to test you, and that His fear may be before you, so that you may not sin." Exodus 20:19-20

Half the problem is religious pastors, and the other half is people who would rather have a leader than a personal relation-ship. We have traded a life of familiarity in place of intimacy. I've talked to people who are afraid to be in the presence of God but okay to be led by a pastor who may or may not know God.

You can see later there is a reason for this. We can't argue God that our ways are okay but we can argue with a man of

God. The Israelites wouldn't argue God face to face but they would argue Moses. They eventually tried to dethrone Moses, until God opened up the ground to judge those who were trying to overthrow Moses. I think sometimes we don't feel as guilty rejecting a man, even if he's from God, than we do God Himself. This is partially why we don't mind taking notes from a man.

"But the anointing which you have received from Him abides in you, and you do not need that anyone teach you; but as the same anointing teaches you concerning all things, and is true, and is not a lie, and just as it has taught you, you will abide in Him." I John 2:27 (NKJV)

I believe the only other reality that motivates people to follow people rather than God is opting out on responsibility. We feel like if the pastor says something, then it's on him. You would be right, if he is wrong, it's on him, but it will also fall onto us. It's not God's will to blindly follow leaders. They must be following the Way. In Acts 17:11 we read this, *"Now these people were more noble-minded than those in Thessalonica, for they received the word with great eagerness, examining the Scriptures daily to see whether these things were so." (NASB)* They were recorded as "noble-minded" or honorable. It's God's will to have teachers, but if we blindly follow any person we can go in the wrong directions. That's exactly how denominations get started. There was a breakthrough in revelation and a group of people loved it, and they wrapped their whole theology around the person who had the revelation, revival, or movement. The problem is, that person was used by God as a disruptor to the current compromise or chaos in His body. It didn't mean that everything that person professed or held in his belief systems came from God. This can be so dangerous.

I've seen so many people follow great pastors when it comes to healing or finances and those people really suffer from wrong teaching. Was he a great pastor? Yes, but did he have revelation or the right perspective on healing? No. You can have the right heart to love people but the wrong perspective. You can have a great revelation on healing and see massive amounts of people healed but not grow a church. You could have all the faith for finances but not have a revelation of purity. This is why we need humility and each other in the body of Christ. I am not good at everything, but I do have revelation on things I'm discussing. I'm ok to admit I haven't grown a megachurch, but I've seen thousands of people healed. I can deliver people from demons but I'm not the best care pastor. I can preach and minister in the Holy Spirit but I'm not the most administrative. We need to be part of the body of Christ, be discipled, but not if it leads to being blinded. As believers, we are supposed to study for ourselves, so we are not fooled by the devil and become ashamed for following the wrong ways for years.[37] This way of thinking doesn't make us lose trust in those who are apostles, prophets, pastors, teachers, and evangelists; it just makes us mature to be able to discern the truth.[38]

There is a place for apostles, prophets, pastors, teachers, and evangelists, but for accountability, teaching, and mobilization. I truly believe God is giving leaders and His body another chance to do what He called us to do. God's intention is for everyone of us to know Him personally and do what He did. He desires intimacy with all of His sons and daughters. Until Jesus comes back, there will always be a place for leaders in the house of

---

37   2 Timothy 2:15
38   Hebrews 5:14

God, but His desire is for them to build maturity in every believer the Way Jesus exemplified.

So many believers are about to be awakened! There is the biggest army of believers awaiting to awaken. These are going to rise to the call of the captain of the Lord of Hosts. I believe COVID got our attention, or should have. A few pastors, leaders, and ministries aren't going to win the game; it's going to be through every believer. I believe in this next wave we will see laymen overtake those who had titles. Not to take over churches or be boastful, but become so free that their fruit goes much further than pastors did before; and they will do it almost accidentally. There is a freedom coming so #Every Believer can move like Jesus intended and invited. The baptism of the Holy Spirit came for power and a bold courage to represent Christ, not primarily for doctrine or to speak in tongues. Yes, I'm in full agreement with the gifts and doctrine of the baptism of the Holy Spirit; however, we must realize that we are limiting God not only to tongues, to be considered Spirit-filled, or even part of a denomination.

We are sitting on a powder keg of God's glory awaiting a shift in perspective. What would happen if those who consider themselves Spirit-filled woke up to the power inside? What would it look like if they all just agreed to walk like Jesus? To believe that they could and should heal the sick? To cast out demons all around? To begin to adopt the world around us in love through discipleship? We could change the world in a matter of years. I believe this is the move of God in the last days. To awaken every believer. Yes, women too! Look, we have to get past this. The Holy Spirit came to empower us. It wasn't about personality, gender, nationality, former religion, or title in a church. Christ's blood saves us all and God's power fills us all.

The following Scriptures reveal the heart of God to pour out upon and through, every believer. As we resubmit our lives to the power of the Holy Spirit for God's purposes, watch how the Holy Spirit begins to encounter you in worship and instrumentally lead you to acts of obedience. This is the power that that turns our every day steps of faith into miracles, life changes, and even destiny!

*"And it shall be in the last days, God says, "That **I will pour out My Spirit on all mankind**; And your sons and your daughters will prophesy, And your young men will see visions, And your old men will have dreams." Acts 2:17 (emphasis mine)*

*"**These signs will accompany those who have believed:** in My name they will cast out demons, they will speak with new tongues; they will pick up serpents, and if they drink any deadly poison, it will not harm them; they will lay hands on the sick, and they will recover." Mark 16:17-18 (emphasis mine)*

"There is neither Jew nor Greek, there is neither slave nor free, there is neither male nor female; for you are all one in Christ Jesus." Galatians 3:28 NASB

*So Jesus said to them again, "Peace be to you; **just as** the Father has sent Me, **I also send you.**" John 20:21 (emphasis mine)*

*And Jesus came up and spoke to them, saying, "All authority in heaven and on earth has been given to Me. Go, therefore, and make disciples of all the nations, baptizing them in the name of the Father and the Son and the Holy Spirit, **teaching*** *them to follow all that I commanded you; and behold, I am with you always, to the end of the age." Matthew 28:18-20 (emphasis mine)*

"and if children, heirs also, heirs of God and fellow heirs with Christ, if indeed we suffer with Him so that we may also be glorified with Him. The Spirit Himself testifies with our spirit that we are children of God." Romans 8:16-17 (emphasis mine)

*But two men had remained in the camp; the name of the one was Eldad, and the name of the other, Medad. And the Spirit rested upon them (and they were among those who had been registered, but had not gone out to the tent), and they prophesied in the camp. So a young man ran and informed Moses, and said, "Eldad and Medad are prophesying in the camp." Then Joshua the son of Nun, the personal servant of Moses from his youth, responded and said, "My lord Moses, restrain them!" But Moses said to him, **"Are you jealous for my sake? If only all the Lord's people were prophets, that the Lord would put His Spirit upon them!"** Numbers 11:26-29 (emphasis mine)*

*John said to Him, "Teacher, we saw someone casting out demons in Your name, and we tried to prevent him because he was not following us." **"Do not hinder him**, for there is no one who will perform a miracle in My name, and be able soon afterward to speak evil of Me. **For the one who is not against us is for us**. For whoever gives you a cup of water to drink because of your name as followers of Christ, truly I say to you, he shall by no means lose his reward." Mark 9:38-40 (emphasis mine)*

3.

THE NECESSITY
FOR THE MIRACULOUS

I was making a regular stop at one of my rental houses. My tenant had half moved out, and I was removing all their belongings in order to clean the house. On one of the trips out of the house I saw our neighbor coming out of her door. I greeted her just like normal, but noticed she looked to be in pain. Soon enough she was communicating her pain to me. She felt she may have been having a heart attack. Her back and chest were hurting at the same time. I had a thought that she was super stressed as well. I asked and she admitted more than normal. Then I took the shot. I said, "Do you want that pain to go away?" She said, "What do you mean?" I replied, "I guarantee you, if you let me pray for you, you will be healed." She replied, "Well, I don't believe in that, I'm an atheist." (Now, I knew this, but unbeknownst to her I had been stepping out seeing a few hundred people healed by now, so I was stoked.) I replied to her, "Then you have nothing to lose if I do pray for you." She said, "Good point." I started to pray and immediately felt the flow of the Holy Spirit touching her. I was getting more and more excited. Typically, what I am sensing is literally being mirrored by what others are sensing. I asked her what she sensed, and to her surprise, she said the pain in her chest and back had gone away suddenly. Now faith was filling this front yard. I sensed the Lord knew her faith was soaring, and He told me to tell her she's about to feel like a liquid oil was going into her soul. I said, "Let me pray for that." She wasn't resistant whatsoever. As I prayed, it felt like liquid peace was flowing out of my soul through the Holy Spirit towards her. After I prayed she said, "It was like you said; liquid peace came in my heart—my anxiety has stopped." I said, "That's because Jesus loves you, Dianne." As we were talking, she said to me, "Twenty minutes ago I was an atheist, but now I believe that there's something. I may not believe like you do, but I believe in you—this was real." Now, for all my religious friends, she wasn't placing faith in me, but felt everything we had been praying. That, my friends, was a win!

It doesn't stop there. Four years later, I'm doing the same thing, cleaning up after a tenant, and while I was making a trip to take things to the curb, she came over to say hi. She said, "I have to tell you something crazy." I said, "I know crazy, I worked for a Spirit-filled Bible College." She said, "I was in my living room and this weird feeling came into the room, like someone was standing there." She said she looked over and there was Jesus standing in the living room." She said He spoke to her and said these words, "I am the Messiah, you can trust in Me." She said at that moment she was born again. Wow! Yay Jesus! One of the biggest moments here was that she was a Jew by heritage before all this, just an Atheist by choice. He had not left her alone. I think it was 6 months later she passed away.

Just think, there was a miracle-shaped hole inside of her heart waiting for a supernatural encounter to fill it. She had a rough life growing up. How many people are like Dianne? There are so many people just like her. Now her story was pretty awesome, but believers and unbelievers are in need of God's supernatural love and power like never before.

I've heard so many believers say things like, "It's better to believe than see," or "The just shall live by faith," when arguing that sinners don't need to experience miracles. Paul says it clearly, "And my speech and my preaching were not with persuasive words of human wisdom, but in demonstration of the Spirit and of power, that your faith should not be in the wisdom of men but in the power of God." I Corinthians 2:4-5

"For our gospel did not come to you in word only, but also in power, and in the Holy Spirit and in much assurance, as you know what kind of men we were among you for your sake." I Thessalonians 1:5

I believe that the lack of miracles is one of the biggest hindrances to people believing. We are proclaiming a supernatural God, and while believing without seeing is good, seeing miracles are biblical and needed. Imagine what's happening in these situations. I get it, there is the odd hater or religious person that Jesus wouldn't have performed a miracle for, but for 99.999999% of people, it's a legitimate need. Think about it; even some of you still have trust issues with God, and it all has to do with a lack for which you hold God accountable. I know we don't say it, but secretly, it's there in so many hearts. I don't know about you, but for me, it takes a lot of evidence for my heart to trust anybody. There are so many fakes out there, saying and doing things that don't work. People are looking for the authentic! They have a real miracle-shaped hole, and if we can help, it will bring about a faith in the God that we preach, the God of the supernatural.

There is a misunderstood story and application that is popular to try and dismiss the need of the supernatural. Before we see a different side of Thomas, I want to challenge how the majority of people use his lack of faith to vindicate a miraculous-less Gospel and Christian life. Thomas was a disciple of the Lord. He had seen thousands of miracles. He had seen Jesus heal every sick person who came to Him, raise dead people, cleanse the lepers, multiply bread and fish at least twice, cast out demons, and more. He had no excuse for his doubt and this is why Jesus rebuked him. EVEN STILL THOUGH, Jesus showed up! No excuses for doubt, but understanding causes compassion to unfold in our hearts, not just for Thomas, but for the whole world.

"Now Thomas, called the Twin, one of the twelve, was not with them when Jesus came. The other disciples therefore said to him, 'We have seen the Lord.' So he said to them, 'Unless I see in His hands the print of the nails, and put my finger into the print of the nails, and put my hand into His side, I will not believe.' And after eight days His disciples were again inside, and Thomas with them. Jesus came, the doors being shut, and stood in the midst, and said, 'Peace to you!' Then He said to Thomas, 'Reach your finger here, and look at My hands; and reach your hand here, and put it into My side. Do not be unbelieving, but believing.' And Thomas answered and said to Him, 'My Lord and my God!' Jesus said to him, 'Thomas, because you have seen Me, you have believed. Blessed are those who have not seen and yet have believed.' " John 20:24-29

We see above the famous part where Thomas was named the doubter by most translators in the subheading. But in reality, Thomas had faith. In the following Scriptures you will see that Thomas spoke up, more than the rest of all the disciples and was willing to die. The Jews had been speaking of stoning Jesus and Thomas volunteered to go die with Christ. I propose that Thomas wasn't always a doubter. I propose that Thomas was sold out. The disciples had sold all and followed Jesus. Most of them, literally. They had left lands and family to follow Jesus. They had sacrificed more than most any of us have known. As you read this passage, you will see the threat of death upon all who may go with Jesus but then the commitment of Thomas even to the place of death.

"Now Jesus loved Martha and her sister and Lazarus. So, when He heard that he was sick, He stayed two more days in the place where He was. Then after this He said to the disciples, 'Let us go to Judea again.' The disciples said to Him, 'Rabbi, lately the Jews sought to stone You, and are You going there again?' " John 11:5-8

"And I am glad for your sakes that I was not there, that you may believe. Nevertheless let us go to him." Then Jesus said to them plainly, "Lazarus is dead. Then Thomas, who is called the Twin, said to his fellow disciples, "Let us also go, that we may die with Him." John 11:14-16

Jesus died. What? Yup. Jesus died and with Him dying, so did Thomas' dream and everything he thought he was living for. Thomas ran into the wall of disillusionment. Again, he was even willing for himself and the disciples to die for the cause, but he wasn't ready for his dream to die.

Thomas, maybe more than the rest of the disciples, was sold out to the cause as much if not more than the others. The problem with the cause was that it was their cause, and not Christ's cause. No matter how many times Jesus told them, their narrative couldn't hear it. They were focused on the OLD mindset and the OLD covenant and not what Jesus came to do. He didn't come to restore Israel; He came to begin the Kingdom of Heaven's explosion. Over and over the disciples kept in their narrative. *"They said to Him, 'Grant us that we may sit, one on Your right hand and the other on Your left, in Your glory.' "* (Mark 10:37 NKJV) or *"Therefore, when they had come together, they asked Him, saying, Lord, will You at this time restore the kingdom to Israel?" (Acts 1:6 NKJV).* They were seeking an old kingdom and they were thinking of their good. They couldn't see that Jesus came to save all.

Just like Thomas, many of us have believed that Jesus came to make our kingdoms better. Jesus came to heal us, protect us, get me married, help my marriage, get me jobs, promote me in life, and truly, get me the American dream. (Wait a sec, isn't this book on the supernatural? Yes. Just wait, this understanding will help heal your heart.) Jesus came to reconcile us with God. He came to take away our sins and the punishment for those sins. Thomas and even some of the disciples had the hardest time seeing this. I believe Thomas wasn't a doubter, he was hurt. His heart had fully given into his version of why Christ was here, and that version died. Yes, Christ coming may eventually help the people of Israel and their captivity but no, that's not why Christ was there. He is literally here in your life to save you from your sin and to empower you within to save others around you. He is here to make us a light to this world. It's bad to say this, but He's not here to give us a good life now, He's here to empower us to be witnesses to Him everywhere we are. He's not concerned if you are happy, He's concerned if you will be with Him now, for eternity, and if He can be with those around us. This world, not one part of it, is our reward. When you think like this, the enemy can't use an out of context Gospel to damage our hearts toward God. Does God provide and do what He says? Yes, but this isn't our purpose nor is it His main priority. I truly believe this is what seeking first His kingdom truly means.[39]

Yes, Thomas could have and should have believed without seeing but Jesus still showed up to Him anyway. Whatever we think Thomas should have believed, maybe there was more to the story than we think. A miracle, that is Jesus showing up to Him, was still allotted by God to confirm Thomas' broken heart. Although it was on Thomas for having an out of context Gospel or promise, Jesus still loved him and showed Himself to Thomas. If Jesus would show up for an established disciple who had seen miracles, don't you think He wants to show up for you and those who have never seen miracles around us? Don't you think He would show up for believers and the lost alike who haven't even come close to the amount of miracles Thomas had seen? Don't you think a body being healed, a word of knowledge about a loved one, or a prophetic word could make or break the sin or doubt cycles some are experiencing? Wouldn't a word of knowledge really make the difference in someone's heart? What if every believer was known to carry God? To carry a word in their heart about someone's situation? Or a prayer for the downtrodden? Or boldness to share the Gospel? Or an other-than-this world kind of love? This is what the world is waiting for.

---

39 Matthew 6:33 NKJV

MIRACLE-SHAPED HOLE IN JOHN THE BAPTIST

I was working a forklift at Fedex for cash to buy all the extra for our kids' activities. While I was there, I was worshipping and praying while working. I remember one day I suddenly, in the Spirit, got a glimpse of a worker, and I saw a vision of him playing keyboard, heard the words "worship leader," and then a follow-up to this with a slight direction. He is playing too many video games, and if he stops and comes back to worship, I'll set some things in his life in order. He had been cursing with everyone else, but I believe he claimed Jesus. I went up to him and asked him if he was or used to be a worship leader, and if he played the keyboard; he looked at me like I smacked him. He said, "Who are you?" I said, "I'm just a believer that hears from God sometimes and God wants you to know He loves you." He said, "I've got to go." He went back to work. In thirty minutes, he came back to me and was like, "So what did you say?" I restated the vision and asked him again. He then said he used to do worship and he does play the keyboard but not anymore. He said he was asking God for direction that very week. Then I cautiously asked him if he plays too many video games, and if, perhaps, it's made him numb in his heart. He said, "Oh my gosh, are you serious?" I answered, "Yes,"—hesitantly. He said shockingly, "I do." I said, "I feel like the Lord is saying for you to put down the video games and pick up worship again, and if you do, He will bring things back together in your life." He was like, "Wow, thank you so much. You don't know how much this means." On the way out of work he ran up to me with more questions. I felt he might have issues with his shoulders and he did. I prayed and both shoulders were healed. God was so amazing! A small vision turns into a big miracle, but this wasn't all. He came and found me two months later. He was about to leave due to a promotion, but wanted to tell me the news. "This weekend I'm going on a worship vigil with my church's worship team and we are writing songs." He was so grateful. He said ever since you gave me that word things started to line up. I just said, "Praise God, He loves you." God's so good and there are so many people willing to come to Christ or back to Christ with a simple word. Even believers!

If John the Baptist needed verification of Jesus being the Messiah, then it's ok that the world needs the miraculous to confirm Jesus is the Way. John the Baptist was sent in the spirit of Elijah to prepare the Way of Jesus. He was in Jail and was about to be beheaded. At this point in your life and ministry, you want to be sure that everything you had lived for was hitting the target. He sent his disciples to go and question Jesus to see if He was the Messiah.

"And when John had heard in prison about the works of Christ, he sent two of his disciples and said to Him, 'Are You the Coming One, or do we look for another?' " Matthew 11:2-3

Just wait a second, didn't John already hear from God that Jesus was the Christ? That He was the Messiah? Yes he did.

"I did not know Him, but He who sent me to baptize with water said to me, 'Upon whom you see the Spirit descending, and remaining on Him, this is He who baptizes with the Holy Spirit. And I have seen and testified that this is the Son of God.' " John 1:33-34

Could it be that the miraculous is needed to help people's faith be in the power of God and not just in great doctrinal presentations. This isn't to qualify doubts but to release the expectation for the miraculous. Jesus' response to John the Baptist disciples is amazing; "And John, calling two of his disciples to him, sent them to Jesus, saying, 'Are You the Coming One, or do we look for another?' When the men had come to Him, they said, 'John the Baptist has sent us to You, saying, Are You the Coming One, or do we look for another?' Jesus answered and said to them, 'Go and tell John the things you have seen and heard: that the blind see, the lame walk, the lepers are cleansed, the deaf hear, the dead are raised, the poor have the gospel preached to them. And that very hour He cured many of infirmities, afflictions, and evil spirits; and to many blind He gave sight. And blessed is he who is not offended because of Me.' " Luke 7:19-23

Jesus literally healed the sick, cast out demons, and performed miracles after John's disciples came for confirmation. Are you serious? Didn't Jesus rebuke the Pharisees demanding a sign? (Matthew 16:1-4) Yes, because their hearts were evil. John's heart was weary. Yes, at the end, just like with Thomas, he added a statement that could be interpreted as correction. But the point is, even though God had already personally spoken to John that Jesus was the Messiah through the sign of the Dove descending upon Jesus, he needed further verification so his heart could settle. Maybe, because of the desert land we have lived through without too many miracles, we have mistakenly commanded that people believe without the supernatural. If John the Baptist had a miracle-shaped hole in his heart, so does the world. Honestly, to win someone's trust is a big deal. With all the media, prosperity tv evangelists, and hypocrisy, it's no wonder we need the miraculous in #Every Believer's life.

THE GOSPEL WAS ALWAYS WITH THE SUPERNATURAL

I was visiting my brother in Canada, and we went to the gym. I struck up a conversation with a huge buff guy about Jesus and he blew me off. Then I decided to target the lady behind the counter. After trying for minutes, bantering back and forth with apologetics and validity for the Gospel, she was getting frustrated and said, "I'd rather believe in Buddha, Muhammed, or run around that tree naked before I believe in Jesus. Show me a miracle and I will believe." I was awestruck. I believed in the miraculous; I had been healed myself. I was healed in my mom's womb miraculously, but at that moment, I was shy. I realized a couple things; she may have believed if I had started with a prayer for healing and, secondly, this is why so many don't believe. Don't get me wrong, the apologetic proof for the Bible, Jesus, and the Word itself SHOULD be enough, but it isn't enough. It wasn't enough for the New Testament believers, so we need this in our lives. For goodness sake, hear what we say, New Testament church. It was the new Way that things were supposed to go. It was the epoch of a new dispensation and that means an expectation of what was supposed to happen. Although this was a seed, I wasn't prepared that day.

All throughout the New Testament, miracles accompanied the Gospel. Whether Matthew 10 or Mark 16, most of the time Jesus sent His disciples to preach the Gospel, it was to heal the sick, cast out demons, and cleanse lepers as well. We see this in the book of Acts that the disciples always functioned with the supernatural in confirmation of the Gospel. On the Island of Malta alone, Paul didn't die from a viper bite and then everyone who was brought to him with any condition was healed. It confirmed the Gospel of Jesus to be the One they could trust. That's why it's stated in Mark 16:16 that these "signs" will follow those who believe, or you could say every believer. Signs are for direction. Everyone is trying to find the way in their life. They all have eternity put in their hearts by God[40] to get the trip started. Just like we have maps and ways to get to certain places, the world is full of false religions or wrong ways to have peace with God; nonetheless, they are there. Signs and wonders literally point the direction in folks' hearts that were placed there by God to turn to Him when they experience them. Even if you have navigation on your car, the signs that mark the roads confirm to your mind or heart where you need to turn. Jesus sent His disciples with the supernatural mandate accompanying them, and He's still sending the supernatural power with believers today.[41]

THE NEW TESTAMENT WAS FULL OF THE SUPERNATURAL

The whole New Testament was full of miracles. It was full of the Gifts of the Holy Spirit, His love, and His power. There are at least twenty individual miracles in the book of Acts as well as nine mentions where multiple miracles happened at once.[42]

Steven, a deacon,[43] was full of the Spirit and wisdom. Look at an unknown guy named Ananais,[44] he literally was having an open vision (gift of the Spirit) about going to Saul, who was about to be Paul, to heal his eyes. Ananais argued with the risen Christ about going. It's a crazy thought—but why argue with Jesus unless you have knowledge of Him? Or perhaps this wasn't

40 Ecclesiastes 3:11
41 Matthew 28:20 NKJV
42 https://ourdailybread.org/resources/the-miracles-of-god-in-acts/
43 Acts 6:5 NKJV
44 Acts 9:10

your first vision? Who knows, but evidently, a normal believer on whom we have no information was used by God in a supernatural way. Aquila and Priscilla are mentioned six times in the New Testament as being powerful.[45] Just think of Peter, Paul, Barnabas, Mark, Phillip, and so many others used by God through the Holy Spirit. So many miracles, so many moves of God, the New Testament has just a small window into what the church had seen and was doing. If they needed the supernatural then, how much more do we need the Holy Spirit now. God's not holding back, let's seek Him for more!

MIRACLES AFTER THE APOSTLES

I was in India with my friend Dan Wilmoth, and we were speaking at several schools a day and doing ministry as the pastor there requested. During one outing, the pastors wanted us to go and pray for a lady who was sick. Upon entering one of the smallest homes I've ever seen, I saw a person who was just bone and flesh. Her sickness kept her from being able to keep any food down so she looked skinnier than some of the commercials to support people in impoverished nations. The pastor started explaining how, when she would go to the hospital, the sickness would leave her and they couldn't find anything wrong with her. Well, without thinking, I said out loud, "It's a demon!" They said "Okay," and I said, "We needed to cast this out." They agreed. I started to pray, and that demon started manifesting. Thankfully, the demon was speaking in their language and not mine, but nonetheless, it eventually came out. She got up after it left, and I told them to feed her right there to test to see if the demon

---

45   Acts 18:2-3; Acts 18-19; Acts 26; Romans 16:3-5; 1 Corinthians 16:19; 2 Timothy 4:19

had gone. She ate and there were no repercussions or nausea. Then we said she had to be born again so that it didn't come back or something worse. They said they led her to Christ later. That was amazing; a spirit could make a lady sick. I know it was Biblical but this was the first time I had seen a healing come by casting out a spirit.

I have seen thousands of immediate healings in the last nine years or so. People in front of me are healed. There have been broken bones healed, arthritis healed, cancers going into recession, growths disappearing, blind eyes opening, deaf ears, and partially deaf hearing again, words of knowledge that brought healing into people, words of knowledge where God gives me names of people I've never known, knees, backs, hips, pain, and so many different miracles; it's been just a privilege to see His power like He's revealed Himself to be.

My brother was miraculously healed. He was supposed to be born an invalid and brain dead, but my mom and the church prayed; he was healed. My mom needed an inner womb blood transfusion when she was pregnant with me; she went to the church and prayed with them again and my blood type changed overnight. My knees were healed at 16-years-old when a healing evangelist came to our church and they haven't hurt since (I'm 42). At the same time I was healed in my knees, all my allergies disappeared. I had four surgeries to get tubes in my ears due to my allergies and was always taking allergy medicine prior to this, so it definitely was a miracle. I believe that my life is a drop in the bucket of the miracles that are supposed to happen, but nonetheless I've seen miracles in my own life. I've known so many people that have had undeniable healings and miracles happen in their lives. You would think that every kind of believer would be the last person to denounce the relativity of miracles but that isn't the truth. The proof of miracles isn't to shame those or correct those who haven't seen miracles, but rather to invite them into the possibility and the pattern to see them.

Even after the Bible was written, the church still saw the miraculous. There were accounts then and even still today. I believe, as we awaken as the body of Christ and take risks to pray for folks, there will be a surge of New Testament miracles invade the earth. My life is just a needle in a haystack of lives with miracles in the world. In fact, they have been happening since creation. Here are a few quotes from early church fathers who saw miracles too:

Justin Martyr (100 AD - 165 AD)

Justin Martyr wrote, "For the prophetic gifts remain with us even to the present time...it is possible to see among us women and men who possess gifts of the Spirit of God." - 'Dialogue with Trypho'

Irenaeus of Lyons in his book, *Against Heresies* (130 AD - 202 AD)

"Men were saved both from most wicked spirits, and from all kinds of demons, and from every sort of apostate power." – 2.6.2

"And so far are they from being able to raise the dead, as the Lord raised them, and the apostles did by means of prayer, and as has been frequently done in the brotherhood on account of some necessity—the entire Church in that particular locality entreating [the boon] with much fasting and prayer, the spirit of the dead man has returned, and he has been bestowed in answer to the prayers of the saints." – 2.31.2

"Wherefore, also, those who are in truth His disciples, receiving grace from Him, do in His name perform [miracles], so as to promote the welfare of other men, according to the gift which each one has received from Him. For some do certainly and truly drive out devils, so that those who have thus been cleansed from evil spirits frequently both believe [in Christ], and join themselves to the Church. Others have foreknowledge of things to come: they see visions, and utter prophetic expressions. Others still heal the sick by laying their hands upon them, and they are made whole. Yea, moreover, as I have said, the dead even have been raised up, and remained among us for many years. And what shall I more say? It is not possible to name the number of the gifts which the Church, [scattered] throughout the whole world, has received from God, in the name of Jesus Christ." – 2.32.4-5

Tertullian (155 AD - 220 AD)

"The clerk of one of them who was liable to be thrown upon the ground by an evil spirit, was set free from his affliction; as was also the relative of another, and the little boy of a third. How many men of rank (to say nothing of common people) have been delivered from devils, and healed of diseases!" – *Scapulam*, 4

Origen (184 AD - 253 AD)

Against Celsus 1.46 – "And there are still preserved among Christians traces of that Holy Spirit which appeared in the form of a dove. They expel evil spirits, and perform many cures, and foresee certain events, according to the will of the Logos. And although Celsus, or the Jew whom he has introduced, may treat with mockery what I am going to say, I shall say it nevertheless

— that many have been converted to Christianity as if against their will, some sort of spirit having suddenly transformed their minds from a hatred of the doctrine to a readiness to die in its defense, and having appeared to them either in a waking vision or a dream of the night."

Against Celsus 1.67 – "And the name of Jesus can still remove distractions from the minds of men, and expel demons, and also take away diseases;"

Cyprian (200 AD - 258 AD)

"And this also is done in the present day, in that the devil is scourged, and burned, and tortured by exorcists, by the human voice, and by divine power;" – Epistle 75, 15

Augustine of Hippo (354 AD –, 430 AD)

"A miracle that happened at Milan while I was there, when a blind man had his sight restored...I have been concerned that such accounts should be published because I saw that signs of divine power like those of the older days were frequently occurring in modern times too...many miracles have occurred there (at Hippo) and to my certain knowledge many miracles have occurred there which are not recorded in the published documents and nearly 70 of these documents have been produced at the time of writing." – *City of God*, 22.8

Vincent Ferrer - (1350 AD - 1419 AD)

There are more that could be mentioned than these. Athanasius, Basel, Gregory of Nazianzus, Gregory of Athansius, Francis of Assisi, Bernard of Clairvaux, Hildegard of Bingen, the Waldenses, Martin Luther (who healed the sick and cast out devils), the Anabaptists, Wesley, and countless others, "Miracles of the Saints,"[46] the book, *Saints Who Raised The Dead*, and many more. People can say they don't believe these instances or even say I made these testimonies up. However, when everyone becomes wrong other than us and our doctrine of Cessationism (that has no Biblical support), it's time to start believing in Jesus once again. Unbelief isn't a trait of believers. Discernment is, yes. I'd rather err on the side of supporting a Biblical God than just a misappropriated theology. The Bible says that we should walk by faith, not by doubt. I know people have claimed miracles that were false and even some in the past were demonic, but let's classify those people as false, not our God who is innately miraculous. Scripture itself is supposed to give faith. It's the life that's still inside the Word that creates an expectancy for miracles. If you read the Bible for yourself, you almost need someone to teach you not to believe in a miraculous God. It's the revelation[47] of Scripture by the power of the Holy Spirit that gives faith. That faith is alive and produces life change and miracles. Why do people spend more time trying to denounce Biblical miracles than they do in actually following a Biblical Jesus? Why are we always looking for reasons to say why healing doesn't work more than why it should work? It is a worldly outlook to take a doubt side of the Biblical worldview. The God of the Bible is miraculous and He didn't just disappear after the original apostles were laid to rest. The Holy Spirit is still in office confirming the works of Jesus to bring people to Christ.

I agree, when people lead others astray with miracles or they themselves lead sinful lifestyles because of miracles, it can be

---

46 website needed here
47 Romans 10:17

dangerous. But can we just say that those people are dangerous and not flowing in the miraculous themselves? Could we as
a body of Christ begin to have discernment and look at the fruit
that begins to follow healings, miracles, deliverances, the power
of the Holy Spirit, and the gifts of the Spirit? Instead of cancelling
the gifts and operations of the Holy Spirit like the church as a
whole has done, I believe it's God's will, that we just stop that
which is misleading and correct those that are in the flesh. The
biggest part about the miraculous, and the need of it was for
the lost. They are all over the place with so many false religions,
claims for contradiction in Christianity, bad examples in the body
of Christ, and more. Miracles have to be the Way for the church
going forward. What's the problem? Much of the body of Christ
has given into a convenient theological outlook called Cessationism or fears the blowback of those who claim it's belief systems.

CESSATIONISM

The subject of continuism or cessationism has divided much of
the body of Christ and really needs a true Biblical approach. Of
course, there are so many arguments for this mentality, but I only
hold a couple thoughts as to why this is not a valid option for
the body of Christ. To even consider that I have all the answers
is boastful and a misguided belief; however this may be, we can
look at dates, facts, and logistical fallacies that empower any believer to minimally feel Biblical about the pursuit of the Holy Spirit Baptism, His power, His supernatural love, and His Gifts. The
Whole Old Testament and New Testament are full of miracles
that point to a miraculous God. The belief of Cessationism says
that miracles ended with the last apostles but there is a problem

with that belief. Miracles never started with the apostles; they started with Creation and have been in every dispensation since then. Not only that, there are thousands of testimonies of current miracles and miracles all throughout church history that reveal God in who He is: a miraculous God. I love this Scripture in the NLT Bible; it says this so plainly, "You are the God who performs miracles; you display your power among the peoples." Miracles aren't simply a dispensation, but Who God really is. *"Jesus Christ is the same, Yesterday, today, and forever." (Hebrews 13:8 NKJV)* and *"For I am the Lord, I change not." (Malachi 3:6a NKJV)*

> "If you were to lock a brand-new Christian in a room with a Bible and tell him to study what the Scriptures have to say about healing and miracles, he would never come out of the room a Cessationist." - Jack Deere (Former Cessationist)

One of Cessantionist's greatest leaders was Benjamin Warfield. He lived from 1821-1921. To his benefit, he was a great defender of Scripture against a liberal movement in that time period. Where he veered off was his book, *Counterfeit Miracles*. Yes, there were some unbiblical miracles happening in the Catholic church, but that just needed clarification and wisdom moving forward. We can't change a miraculous God or the Word just to stop people from believing a wrong thing. That's a wrong trying to cancel out another wrong, and the crazy thing is, it was too late. Legitimate miracles had been already happening and have happened since then. It's impossible to keep a miraculous God inside of a man-made theology. Yes, I truly believe that miracles are to bring a witness in the courtroom of every heart that Jesus is the Messiah and also to encourage believers in the strength of their walk. I don't believe in "showism," fake miracles, or demonic miracles that include a stigmata with Christ's death upon its people. This has no basis in the New Testament for any of its claims. But I don't believe in denouncing miracles just because there have been sects of denominations that misuse it. I'd rather say that people are off than change the Word and say God isn't miraculous or do miracles.

For this to be true there would have to be substantial Biblical evidence of which there isn't. The fact that Jesus said, "teaching men to observe everything I've commanded you until the end of the age"[48] should say it all. That is, if we are followers of Jesus and not a denominational seminary. Dropping any name in competition with Jesus is heresy at its root. Jesus is the trump card for the name above every other name, not just metaphorical, hyperbolic, or symbolic measures, but taking Him real how He said.

AT SOME POINT, JESUS HAS TO COME INTO OUR THEOLOGY.

One of the books Cessationist uses is called *Sola Scriptura*. They thought that having the gifts of Apostles and gifts of the Spirit would lessen the authority of Scripture. The problem is, miracles and the gifts weren't to write Scripture but to reach the lost with tangible miracles and to encourage the Body in the Scriptures. It was to validate Scripture and not to change it. Again, I understand that there were people challenging Scriptures but the wrong thing to do is to create a Theology out of need rather than revelation. The Scriptures are authored by God, and it was evident during church history that books were inspired by the

---

48 Matthew 28:20 NKJV

multiplicities of use and inspiration in connection with the Old Testament.

The last thing I will mention about Cessationism is its focus. Its focus was on the inside. Every time the church focuses on the inside it starts to lose its purpose. The very essence of the Gospel is the GO. The very essence of the baptism of the Holy Spirit was to empower disciples to give witness to the resurrection of Jesus Christ through power. It was for expansion into the whole world. Cessationists use 1 Corinthians 13:10: "But when the perfect comes, the partial will pass away." They think this meant the Bible for the church. But that's not even Scriptural. Miracles bring attention to the Way, Jesus. Jesus told Nicodemus in John 3:3 that you must be born again to see the Kingdom of God. That means the text of the Scripture can only be understood by those who are born again. The Bible says, *"The god of this world has blinded them."* 2 Corinthians 4:4 (NKJV). It can take a miracle or supernatural sign to break that blindness that is over people's eyes. I've said this before, but the currency of trust in people's hearts is huge, and God knows this and shows signs to convince them to trust. It says in Romans 8:32 (NKJV), "If God didn't withhold His own Son, how much more would He freely give us all things." Jesus already came, then miracles aren't anything for God to win the lost with. I get it, this is also why Calvinism is ramped in the church. People are fearful to share the Gospel with just the Word, or even tiresome so they invent another belief that God controls everything. But this would be outrageous. That would say that the nations who are the most unreached are because God has not sent people to reach them? Is He racist? Like He's not after Chinese or Indian people? I know the Middle East is growing with more salvations, but maybe God didn't want them saved now? Are the ones who supposedly claim to protect Scripture changing it? The Bible says, *"God wishes that none would perish but all could come to repentance." 2 Peter 3:9 NKJV.* If God is just in control of things then why disciple like Jesus said, or preach the Gospel to every creature?[49] All of these doctrines are just for the comforting of "us four and no more" and not with the mind of Christ.

There are still miracles, and Jesus is the secret weapon to understand the foundation for #Every Believer to walk in the miraculous. I want to encourage you to believe again. It's Jesus through you that's powerful and although we change, He remains the same. I'm praying that while you are reading this book, God's power will change you and release your heart to believe for the miraculous. I'm believing for you to get boldness and faith to step out for Christ like never before.

---

49   Mark 16:15-18

4.

JESUS, THE SECRET WEAPON

As I was leading the transition from worship to preaching, I saw her entering the sanctuary. This time, she was not as normal. Ruby Morgan was a regular face at our church and just had a severe stroke. As she walked very slowly with her walker, I heard the Holy Spirit say to go and pray for her. By this point, I had learned not to delay. I dropped the mic and speedily walked toward Ruby. As I got closer I greeted her and showed her compassion. I asked what was happening in her body. She said she had a stroke and her left side was left almost completely paralyzed. I asked her if she wanted it to go away. She replied, "Of course, and I believe." I really felt the compassion and faith of the Lord rise up in me. I began to pray and immediately I felt this great anointing begin to flow through me. Jesus was moving. As I was praying she started moving. I kept feeling more of God's presence flowing through me. I asked her, "What are you feeling, Ruby?" She said, "I feel the power of God." I said, "Are you getting movement back on the side that was paralyzed?" She said, "It's beginning to have movement again!" I was ecstatic! Wow, a miracle is happening right here. Soon enough, in a matter of minutes, she received full mobility in what was paralyzed! This was amazing.

"But we speak the wisdom of God in a mystery, the hidden wisdom which God ordained before the ages for our glory, which none of the rulers of this age knew; for had they known, they would not have crucified the Lord of glory." I Corinthians 2:7-8

The revelation of Jesus is the key to flowing in the power of Heaven. I believe this revelation, second to His Atonement, is the biggest missing key to the body of Christ today. This one revelation has changed everything for me. It has released the availability of my faith in God's power toward everyone we pray for. Miracles started happening when I realized this. Jesus truly is the secret weapon for #Every Believer and the world alike. It is the reason why there is a worldwide rejection of Christianity and His name from public platforms and even in private meetings.

Jesus has been the secret weapon since the beginning. He is the Word and everything in the Word points to Him. It's all about Jesus. The enemy knows this and has hidden or tried to block Jesus various times. During Jesus' miraculous birth, Herod put out a decree to kill all children under two years of age[50] near Bethlehem. Once Jesus did die and rose from the grave, and although they knew His resurrection to be true, they lied about it so nobody would believe His story (Matthew 28:11-15 NKJV). You have to know the Pharisees were ruled by Satan. They knew of it yet covered it. They covered God's story. Even to this day, they cover God's story of redemption, that is, of the Messiah. The Rabbi's who teach according to the Bible purposely skip Isaiah 53 and dismiss the overwhelming prophecies of Christ Himself or Jesus life fulfilled.[51] It caused so much confusion because it

---

50 Matthew 2:16-18
51 https://www.newtestamentchristians.com/bible-study-resources/351-old-testament-prophecies-fulfilled-in-jesus-christ/

undeniably depicted the sufferings Christ went through, so they stopped teaching it.

Jesus is the Way. I used to think this was symbolism or a prayer to pray for salvation only, but this was God manifesting Himself through Christ to give us the pattern for all believers to follow. After He died, it was limitless. His message and His power was through every believer. Yes, He was the only Way to receive forgiveness of sin but John 14 was talking about more than this. They didn't listen to the prophets so God sent His Son. He came down Himself through the life of His Son to reveal Himself and His will in the clearest Way He had ever communicated. Jesus was God in the flesh.[52] He wasn't just a one-time show to wow the masses but God Himself setting up the New Testament and setting a New Way for His followers to walk in. He meant for us to listen to Jesus. Jesus said a greater One was clearly here, speaking about Himself.[53] We were to take Him more seriously than all the others that had gone before. He was the One they all spoke of, and everything is and was about Him; so why, since He is here, do we not take His Word seriously? Why is it that the clearest revelation of Jesus came, but yet we try to "dispensationalize" Jesus, His works, and His ways? Wasn't Revelation to show that the greatest One was among us? That His Words, ways, and life were to be followed? We have capped or limited the ways of Jesus to only Him and His disciples when He said to train men how He trained the disciples UNTIL He comes back.[54] Jesus is the Way and walking in His power is possible. I pray our hearts would open to this best kept secret.

---

52 John 1:14
53 Matthew 12:42-43; Luke 11:31-32
54 Matthew 28:20

"Therefore still having one son, his beloved, he also sent him to them last, saying, 'They will respect my son.'" Mark 12:6 NKJV

"God, who at various times and in various ways spoke in time past to the fathers by the prophets, has in these last days spoken to us by His Son, whom He has appointed heir of all things, through whom also He made the worlds; who being the brightness of His glory and the express image of His person, and upholding all things by the word of His power, when He had by Himself purged our sins, sat down at the right hand of the Majesty on high." Hebrews 1:1-3 NKJV

JESUS WAS NOT JUST A PRAYER TO PRAY, BUT A LIFE TO LIVE.

"Is there an aunt Mary here with a cervical condition?" It was a Wednesday night service and we were growing in words of knowledge. I had seen God come through a few times but was still quite nervous. I heard the name "Aunt Mary, who has a cervical condition" so I took the jump. A lady who is one of our assistant pastors said she had an Aunt Mary but didn't think she had a cervical condition. Oh my gosh, now the pressure was on. Did I miss it? I kept on with a couple smaller words of knowledge I had, and she said she would call her aunt. It wasn't until after the service she got ahold of her aunt and come to find out she had suffered from a cervical issue for the last twenty years! Praise Jesus! The word really ministered to her aunt, as I believed the intent wasn't to wow the people in the service but heal her aunt. We did share it later as a testimony, and this encouraged the body. This is why we must believe in the Jesus Way and take risks when we see needs or sense the promptings of the Holy Spirit.

Jesus was the purest form of God more than anybody else; He was God. We see glimpses of God, names of God, the law of God, some of the heart of God, but not God fully and completely. Jesus was the fullness of God completely. He was the image of God we need to see. He is the Way of God unfolded. He was the epoch of a New Way for God's people—#Every Believer. He was the New Testament, New Covenant, the New Normal, and a New Epoch.

A "new normal" is a phrase we have become accustomed to since COVID hit the world. Jesus, though, was supposed to stay the new normal. The history of religion since Jesus came is evident. It made Jesus, His Way, and His power just a season and not the New Normal for every believer. When He displayed the will of the Father for every believer, He was literally saying this is the Way it is to be from now on. As you read, pay attention to the dialogue in some of the Scriptures. Seeing Jesus how He displayed His Father and Himself for us to follow, is everything in seeing the supernatural regularly in our lives.

JESUS WASN'T JUST A ONE-TIME SHOW TO WOW THE MASSES, BUT A PATTERN FOR #EVERY BELIEVER TO FOLLOW.

"And if I go and prepare a place for you, I will come again and receive you to Myself; that where I am, there you may be also. And where I go you know, and the way you know." Thomas said to Him, "Lord, we do not know where You are going, and how can we know the way?" Jesus said to him, "I am the way, the truth, and the life. No one comes to the Father except through Me." "If you had known Me, you would have known My Father also; and from now on you know Him and have seen Him." Philip

83

said to Him, "Lord, show us the Father, and it is sufficient for us."
Jesus said to him, "Have I been with you so long, and yet you
have not known Me, Philip? He who has seen Me has seen the
Father; so how can you say, 'Show us the Father?' Do you not
believe that I am in the Father, and the Father in Me? The words
that I speak to you I do not speak on My own authority; but the
Father who dwells in Me does the works. Believe Me that I am
in the Father and the Father in Me, or else believe Me for the
sake of the works themselves." "Most assuredly, I say to you,
he who believes in Me, the works that I do he will do also; and
greater works than these he will do, because I go to My Father."
John 14:5-12.

Look, even Jesus' disciples didn't see Jesus as the Way.
Don't feel bad! They thought His ways were a great suggestion,
but they wanted Him to be about their day politics and were
wondering when He'd be king of Israel. When are you going
to make our nation a nation again? He who has an ear let them
hear. Even by the time He rose from the grave, they WERE STILL
sold out on THEIR country rather than HIS MISSION. It was so
much so, when He was talking in Acts 1, they were still focused
on Israel becoming a nation again or "great again." His own disciples didn't get it until He LEFT their mission, went to His place,
and then sent them His Holy Spirit so they could see what He
saw, from the inside. The church today is still in the Dark Ages
spiritually. They are waiting for Him to repair our nations rather than serve in His mission. We've regressed. Jesus is still the
Way!

'Gathering them together, He commanded them not to
leave Jerusalem, but to wait for what the Father had promised,

"Which," He said, "you heard of from Me; for John baptized with water, but you will be baptized with the Holy Spirit not many days from now." So, when they had come together, they began asking Him, saying, "Lord, is it at this time that You are restoring the kingdom to Israel?" But He said to them, "It is not for you to know periods of time or appointed times which the Father has set by His own authority; ' Acts 1:4-7.

This dialogue was with His disciples who had been with Him for some time already. As we had mentioned, they hadn't understood that they were actually and literally supposed to copy His example. Just as these disciples were with Him but still NOT taking Him seriously, we can be with Jesus but NOT understand that He was the EPOCH of a new way. This, I believe, is the state of many in the church. Jesus is a way, but not THE Way we conduct our lives. There is no condemnation, but there is need for an awakening in our hearts and theology. Jesus has to be our theology if He is our Way.

THEOLOGY IS THAT WHICH WE TAKE SERIOUSLY.

So many believers SEEM to have sound doctrine but not sound action. We forget that Jesus said it is a foolish man who hears His Words55 and doesn't do them. He didn't say the wise would create impeccable doctrine that makes them feel safe. Although it does have a place (1 Timothy 4:16, 6:20), it was not the focus of Christ nor His primary instruction. It was to obey HIS commands.

Look further into this dialogue. Thomas said, *"Lord, we do not know where You are going, and how can we know the way?" (vs 4)* Even though Jesus had shown them the WAY TO FOLLOW,

55 Matthew 7:23-27

85

they had not taken Him seriously. Jesus was explaining that He wasn't just a prayer to pray, but a life to follow, and an expectancy from the Father to move in. Jesus was showing them the Way. Wow! Most Christendom isn't following Jesus other than a prayer to pray. His Way was never to stop. Imagine this! We are hoping and praying for the latter rain; we are wondering WHY the ministry of the Spirit ISN'T seeming to show more glory than the ministry of death, but still don't take His ministry as the revelation of heaven for every believer. Jesus said, "the traditions of man make the power of God of no effect (Mark 7:13 Note). That means you and me. Wow, just like these disciples, we may have enlisted in narratives that don't include Jesus as the full revelation of God, as the Way to follow. We are not seeing His lifestyles as the will of God unfolded in living color for us to follow.

Then Phillip said, *"Lord, show us the Father, and it is sufficient for us."* He still didn't get it after Jesus answered Thomas. Don't worry, if believers who walked with Him didn't get it, it's okay if we haven't seen this. Culture plays a huge part. We grow up trusting those around us to interpret both life and more importantly, God, for us. The problem is, if our parents and those we trust, including pastors, preach a different Gospel or a different possibility, this can lead to our adopting a less than Christ-centered discipleship. I've met so many believers who don't know God, who He is, or His will for their life. It's so much easier to look for other Ways to define God's will in and through us. What's God's will for my life? Is it God's will to heal me? Is it God's will to deliver me? Is it God's will to use me? Really? It's because Jesus has no part of their theology.

JESUS WOULDN'T HAVE ASKED US TO DO THE SAME WORKS BUT GIVEN US A LESSER VERSION OF THE HOLY SPIRIT.

Jesus wouldn't have told us to do the same works He had done and given us a lesser version of the Holy Spirit. It was the power of the Holy Spirit that Jesus functioned in. Many believers I hear say, "Well, that was Jesus" as if it's out of our range of possibility to follow in His steps. Jesus exemplified everything as a human, not functioning as God. He was baptized in water and didn't need to be; He was baptized in the Spirit and didn't need to be if He was acting as God. Jesus became a human, so humans could follow His Way. *"Have this mind among yourselves, which is yours in Christ Jesus, who, though he was in the form of God, did not count equality with God a thing to be grasped, but made himself nothing, taking the form of a servant, being born in the likeness of men." Philippians 2:5-7.* Jesus became a man so He could die as an innocent man for all of us guilty men. He also became a man to encourage us that it's God's will for God to work through #Every Believer as He did through Christ. This was the meaning of John 14:4-12. Jesus literally told the disciples that the reason they can have confidence to do the same works and even greater works was because it was the Father doing the works. If the Father did it through Him, He will do it through us.

MIRACLES START WITH THE SPIRIT

Do you realize that Jesus did no miracles until the power of the Holy Spirit came upon Him after He was baptized? Jesus literally was walking this out as a man for us to have faith to do the same works as men and women anointed with the Holy Spirit. This next Scripture was after Jesus had received the Spirit. The Holy

Spirit is that which qualifies us to move for God. Jesus started His ministry after receiving the Holy Spirit.

*"**The Spirit of the Sovereign Lord is on me,** because the Lord has anointed me to proclaim good news to the poor. He has sent me to bind up the brokenhearted, to proclaim freedom for the captives **and release from darkness for the prisoners."** Luke 4:18 (Emphasis mine)*

Some would say that the advantage Jesus had was a perfect relationship with the Father, and there was no sin. They would be right. The thing that extends that very same blessing to us is His death and resurrection. When Jesus died on our behalf, any separation between us and God died as well. The Bible says that we are joint heirs with Jesus.[56] Now, we know this has nothing to do with our own works, but His works. Many think that if we say that we can do the same works Jesus did, or that we have the same Holy Spirit He had, it's belittling Jesus, but it's not; it's actually bringing glory and truth to His name. The Bible said that He humbled Himself like a man.[57] That means He was God but walked and limited Himself as a man would need to. He even said that He couldn't do anything on His own.[58] This was the whole reason for His dialogue with His disciples in John 14. It gives faith to a man to know you were set up for success and not defeat. You have access to the same power Christ had—if He's asking you to do the same works. We have the same Father backing us up that Jesus had backing Him up.[59] Jesus was simply illustrating how we were to walk, and how possible it was to walk as believers, and not how hard it was to walk as He did.

56 Romans 8:17 NKJV
57 Philippians 2:5-7 NKJV
58 John 5:30 NKJV
59 John 20:21; John 14:1-6 NKJV

This messes so many people up, but this is the proof of how we truly see Jesus as God. We should listen to what He said, and not try to make everything He did as sacred, holy, and limited to only Him. Jesus never said to worship Him nor do we see the disciples worshiping Him after every miracle. Yes, they should have worshiped Him, but He didn't come to be worshiped; He came to live and die for us to be saved and to follow in His footsteps. He also saw obedience to His commands as love more than just the worship of lips.[60]

IT WAS GOD IN CHRIST REVEALING HIMSELF

I was leading a church service in the Philippines and our team and I were praying for people who wanted to be healed. I saw a blind lady from across the room and the Holy Spirit whispered to me, "You have faith to heal her." I crossed the room to pray for her. I asked her (some people actually resist prayer) if she wanted to be healed and she said yes. I started praying for her healing. As I was praying I could sense the Holy Spirit touching her, and after a while, I stopped and asked her if anything was happening. (I do this because our hearts are looking for what God may be doing. That helps create faith for more if anything is happening). She said she was starting to see a white light, like a dot of light beginning to form. I responded, "This is good, God breaking through."Her interpreter told her, and I kept praying for her and every time I stopped, there was more happening and then finally, "breakthrough!" She was healed. The interpreter said she could see! I said "Praise God!" She continued to interpret for the lady. "She said to say thank you, she thinks you're handsome, and you have a big nose!" Wow, she really could

60 Luke 6:46; John 14:15; Matthew 15:8

see! It's funny, but in the Philippines they are not as sensitive; this surprised me, but really showed me she could now see! What a breakthrough!

"That is, that God was in Christ reconciling the world to Himself, not imputing their trespasses to them, and has committed to us the word of reconciliation." II Corinthians 5:19 (NKJV)

The Revelation of God is so amazing through the life of Jesus. He was the fullest revelation of God's nature for us, through us, and for the world. God has used this Scripture to bring clarity. *"God was in Christ reconciling the world to himself." (2 Corinthians 5:19 (NKJV).* Wow, that means it was actually God working through Jesus and not just Jesus on His own mission. This changes everything. This affirmed my revelation of John 14. I could read this Scripture over and over and all of a sudden I saw it. How God was in Christ healing every sick person who came to Him. How God was in Christ casting out demons. How God was in Christ revealing Himself through Christ's life! How God was in Christ revealing His perfect will for #Every Believer to follow! Jesus said, "He could do nothing on His own," but this made it clear. Jesus was only doing what the Father showed Him. Jesus was only speaking what the Father asked. Jesus was only doing the Father's will. God was in Christ, not Christ was in Christ doing a one time show. God was in Christ revealing the Way for believers to walk, showing them His Will through Christ's action and His sacrifice. Healing the sick was God's idea. Casting out demons was the Father's idea. Making disciple's was God's idea. That's why Jesus said if you believe in Me, in context of His Works being the Father's will, we would do the same works and even greater because He had to go.

So Jesus said to them again, "Peace to you! As the Father has sent Me, I also send you." John 20:21

GOD NEVER SENT YOU EMPTY HANDED.

When Jesus said we would do the same works it was because He knew that heaven would back us as much as it did Him. It wasn't because He was a one-time show but an example for all believers to expect. When Jesus said, "As the Father has sent Me, I also send you," He wasn't just talking about the act of preaching the Gospel. He was promising the power of ambassadorship. He was setting in place, before Heaven and Hell, those who would receive His mandate as Ambassadors to set up His kingdom in this world. As much as He was sending, He was promising support. In essence He was saying, "Just as the Father backed Me, I'll back You." "As the Father anointed Me, I'll anoint you." "As the Father was with Me, I'll be with you." "As the Father spoke to me, I'll speak to you." Hold on, I'm not putting words He never spoke as the Word but I am proving a point, He'd never ask us to do the same works and give us a lesser version of the Holy Spirit. He never sent us empty handed! You can see a sending yes but a fully supported sending from Jesus. He is behind us to do the same things He did, and greater!

SOME KIND OF THEOLOGY

Theology is a big word. To me it means, "that which I take serious about God." Or we could say, that which we apply in our lives. How many actually take Jesus into their theology? It simply means the study of God or as I like to say—how I see God in my life. If it's real, it's important we get it right. If the understanding of God determines what we receive from God, then it's pertinent we understand God. I want to challenge you that most of the established church doesn't cling to God as Jesus in its theology, but mostly just for our forgiveness or a ticket to Heaven. In this section, I want to re-introduce theology; that is, the Way to expect from God in our personal lives through the person of Jesus. This has changed everything for me. It's crazy to even say it like that because most believers will think they believe in Jesus as their theology, but as you read, I promise you, He's not.

What's God's will on healing? Jesus. What's God's Way on marriage? Jesus. What's God's will on deliverance? Jesus. What's God's will for discipleship? Jesus. What's God's will for every believer? Jesus. I know, I know—people will say that Jesus was just for the disciples, but that's not even correct hermeneutics. Jesus said, "Teaching them to observe everything I've commanded you." It wasn't just for the disciples. Nor was it just a time dispensation. This Scripture sets that narrative straight; Jesus was the Way, until He comes back.

*"And Jesus came up and spoke to them, saying, "All authority in heaven and on earth has been given to Me. Go, therefore, and make disciples of all the nations, baptizing them in the name of the Father and the Son and the Holy Spirit, **teaching them to follow all that I commanded you**; and behold, I am with you always, to the end of the age." Matthew 28:18-20 (emphasis mine)*

JESUS AS THE WAY TO KNOW GOD

Believers don't see Jesus as the will of God for healing, as the will of God for making disciples, as the will of God for sonship, as the will of God for provision, or the will of God FOR EVERY BELIEVER.

Jesus was literally telling HIs disciples who should have known, but didn't, that He was the Way to heal the sick, He was the Way for discipleship, He was the Father's will. He was telling them that everything He was doing was literally SHOWING THEM and all believers the NEW NORMAL we were to expect as believers. He wasn't just a one time show to wow the masses but the example to FOLLOW AND EXPECT from the Lord.

Salvation only! Salvation has become the only dependence in our narrative of faith when it comes to Jesus. We have traditionally ONLY looked to Him as the Way to the Father when it comes to our salvation. What I want to grab your attention to is this: we should have carried our EXPECTATIONS passed forgiveness of sins INTO EVERY WAY to receive from the Father.

"He who did not spare His own Son, but delivered Him over for us all, how will He not also with Him freely give us all things?" Romans 8:32

IT IS WRONG to hold our view of Jesus as only our forgiveness for our sins. He was to be our example for everything. Jesus was the WAY to discipleship, to deliverance, to giving, and respectively, to HEALING, and to everything.

"Jesus is the Same Yesterday, Today, & Forever" - Hebrews 13:8.

The Son of God appeared for this purpose, to destroy the works of the devil. 1 John 3:8

"For the Law was given through Moses; grace and truth were realized through Jesus Christ. No one has seen God at any time; the only begotten God who is in the bosom of the Father, He has explained Him." John 1:17-18

THE FOUNDATION OF THE CHURCH

I want us to look at the next passage of Scripture to build upon the former revelation. In this passage, Jesus' Disciples are asked by Him who people think He is. Everyone has heard what others say but only Peter has revelation of who Christ is. This is so crucial. Context is everything. Could it be that Christ was telling Peter that the "Rock" that would be the cornerstone of the church was the revelation that Jesus was God? That this was the clearest revelation of God and the key that would open the power of God to move through every disciple? That maybe, this revelation of Jesus being the Way, not just a prayer to pray, but all the Words He would say, and the life that He exemplified? Jesus is showing in John 14 and in this passage and many others that He was setting up the New Testament.

*"Now when Jesus came into the region of Caesarea Philippi, He was asking His disciples, "Who do people say that the Son of Man is?" And they said, "Some say John the Baptist; and others, Elijah; and still others, Jeremiah, or one of the other prophets." He *said to them, "But who do you yourselves say that I am?" Simon Peter answered, "You are the Christ, the Son of the living God." And Jesus said to him, "Blessed are you, Simon Barjona, because flesh and blood did not reveal this to you, but My Father who is in heaven. **And I also say to you that you are Peter, and upon this rock I will build My church;** and the gates of Hades will not overpower it. I will give you the keys of the*

kingdom of heaven; and whatever you bind on earth shall have been bound in heaven, and whatever you loose on earth shall have been loosed in heaven." Matthew 16:13-19 (emphasis mine)

This is what sets Christianity apart. That God became flesh.[61] Jesus wasn't another prophet and He wasn't an earthly King. He was the everlasting Father, and the Prince of Peace revealing Himself clearly. He was God incarnate bringing the perfect will for men to follow. This was the New Testament that God was bringing into awareness. God becoming flesh. How could a 4D God communicate to 3D people? He had to become 3D. We couldn't see it perfectly through the Old Testament so God now CLEARLY explains Himself through the life of His Son, Yeshua.

The early church got this. They continued His ministry with power. Read Acts and other historical documents of the early church. They took Jesus seriously and they took Jesus literally, and it worked! I believe we still read Jesus' Words and see His life like a one-time show, but He came to set up the new Way. He was the "new normal." The church followed this pattern and turned the known world upside down.

Why are we not seeing success in the body of Christ? We have come up with ways that don't require His power and don't produce the same fruit. Jesus works but to see His line of power, love, and service is not convenient. To see it, we cannot be needs based, me based, or any other kind of blessing.

JESUS WAS EVERYTHING

Philip was saying to Jesus, "Show us the Father and it's sufficient to us." (John 14). In Jesus' revelation, Philip was neither

61   John 1:14

seeing Jesus as the "Everlasting Father," nor as His Way, nor the weight of His Words. It looked like Thomas, Philip, and the others were looking only to Jesus as a cute Messenger, and in their expectation, that He would make Israel a nation again. They did not see Him as the King of Kings, or Lord of Lords, or the Father setting up a new Way for people to walk in.

Jesus was setting them up by asking who men say He is. However we accept Jesus is how he works in our lives. What? Yes, if I honor you as a prophet, I get a prophet's reward. If I honor you as a friend I may get a friend's reward. If I honor you as my boss, I'll get a boss' reward...if you are a good boss. However we Honor Christ is how we receive from Him but mostly how we serve Him.

"For the law was given through Moses, but grace and truth came through Jesus Christ. No one has seen God at any time. The only begotten Son, who is in the bosom of the Father, He has declared Him." John 1:17-18

The disciples had not honored Jesus how He truly was. He was the Way to a New Life for believers. His Words were not just radical or cute, but in them was eternal life. He wasn't just another prophet, but who the prophets said would come. He wasn't just a King for Israel but the King of Kings. They hadn't taken Him seriously. Look at Thomas' response in John 14:5, *"Thomas said to Him, 'Lord, we do not know where You are going, and how can we know the way?'"* Although Jesus had shown them the Way, they hadn't been taking notes. Even to the place in the first chapter of Acts where again they were still thinking of their Narrative and not His Way. How many times do we want Christ to suit the narrative or our life and not His Way He set up?

HONOR IS EVERYTHING

"He who receives a prophet in the name of a prophet shall receive a prophet's reward. And he who receives a righteous man in the name of a righteous man shall receive a righteous man's reward." Matthew 10:41

So He said to them, "When you pray, say: Our Father in heaven, Hallowed be Your name. Your kingdom come. Your will be done On earth as it is in heaven." Luke 11:2

Just think, Jesus' disciples had seen Jesus heal everyone who came to Him, cast out all demons that came to Him, everyone He prayed for to raise from the dead raised, every leper cleansed, the broken hearted healed, and more. They were so convinced that God heard His prayers. Why do people ask successful people how they got the results they did? Because they want to implement success. These disciples were hungry. If you read the Lord's prayer above I think we overlook one thing, *"Hallowed be Your Name."* This means "revered" or "Holy" is Your name. The Bible says, "The secret of the Lord is to those who fear God." (Psalms 25:14) It's no secret that Christ revered His Father. One of the biggest keys in believers lives is that Christ or even God, is just another way, just another thought, an addition. God deserves all of our praise and all of our obedience. Powerful prayer happens when a submissive heart approaches. We don't approach God because He should have done something, could have done something, or just because of the irritation of the situation, but because we revere Him. We honor Him over our own Ways. I believe the positioning of this portion of the prayer was strategic by Christ. Get your life in line with His, and heaven begins to open. I believe this is HUGE strategy of the enemy. Familiarity with Jesus and God can create a seemingly bronze heaven. A contrite, or submissive heart[62] causes God to come to the rescue. What? Yup. Reverence is key.

At the beginning of our marriage, we got a book called, *Love and Respect*. It basically states that women need to be loved and men need to be respected. It went as far to say that men would rather be respected than told they are loved. My wife was taken aback, "Surely this isn't true, is it Greg?" "Yup, I'd rather be respected rather than told I'm loved all day long." She was in unbelief. The crazy thing is, God is the same. His secrets are to those who take Him seriously, those who fear Him. He says things like, *"They honor me with their mouth but their heart is far from Me." Matthew 15:8, Isaiah 29:13 NKJV),* and *"Why do you call Me Lord Lord, but don't do what I say," (Luke 6:46 NKJV)* and more. Taking Jesus' Word seriously is revering the literal face of God.

Jesus wasn't just another Way but **the** Way. If we look back to Matthew 16, His disciples mentioned who people thought He was, such as another prophet or way of life. Jesus was purposely bringing the subject up so they could see who He was and would awaken to take His Words seriously. He was trying to bring distinction and evidently was prompted to do this knowing Peter had the revelation for the rest of the disciples to hear.

I travel quite a bit, have pastored for over ten years, and share my faith with most people I meet. People look at Jesus in different ways. I have to be honest though, most people look to Him on how He suits a physical need or benefits them and not

---

62 Psalm 57:17

as God. Most people don't have the line of respect for Christ or His Words as God. Now, this is new and old. It is intended to awaken our souls from a sleep and a dishonor we have been in. If we honor Christ as a friend, He may, if we are lucky, be a friend. If we honor Christ as the provider, He may be, if we are lucky, the provider. If we honor Him as Savior, we get Him as Savior. But if we honor Him as God, we get all the rest. The problem with Jesus being God is this, we have to change. His Ways must now become ours. I believe we have, as a body, embraced the benefits of Jesus for our lives but not the God part that was supposed to govern our lives. He has become a one-sided Jesus. It's where we pick and choose which part of Jesus we like or what aides us at the moment. There is nothing wrong with the benefits side but the God side and the possibilities are miraculous; His Words were supposed to bear more weight in our lives than our desires.

"That all should honor the Son just as they honor the Father. He who does not honor the Son does not honor the Father who sent Him." John 5:23

Jesus wasn't just the prophet of the house, He was the House.[63] Moses was a prophet who built the house. If Moses had weight on His teaching how much more weight should we place on Jesus Ways and words.

"Therefore we must give the more earnest heed to the things we have heard, lest we drift away. For if the word spoken through angels proved steadfast, and every transgression and disobedience received a just reward, how shall we escape if we neglect so great a salvation, which at the first began to

---

63 Hebrews 3:3

be spoken by the Lord, and was confirmed to us by those who heard Him." Hebrews 2:1-3

So many believers are in a less-than-Old Testament mindset and wondering why they don't receive New Testament benefits. It's all in our mindsets and hearts. I believe that sometimes we want the blessing of Abel but only give the sacrifice of Cain. We want salvation, protection, family unity, houses, cars, etc. but don't want the sacrifice or cost of what Jesus takes. Even when it comes to standing for Jesus' Way for His benefits, if we truly believe it, we are regularly looking to bless people with Him, and not just holding to our own. I know, this isn't popular or comfortable, but it is His Way.

"For the law was given through Moses, but grace and truth came through Jesus Christ. No one has seen God at any time. The only begotten Son, who is in the bosom of the Father, He has declared Him." John 1:17-18

LOOKING THROUGH A GLASS WINDOW

I grew up always having food on the table and a roof over my head, but not having what many other kids had. Sometimes it was like looking through a glass window at all the other kids. Maybe one day I could have this and that. I was never jaded, but always thought it would be nice to have some things some day. I believe the body of Christ is like this. So many people are living a less-than-Old Testament version of Christianity but declaring the latter glory. What? Yes. I mean, some of the things people repeat are words the prophets didn't even say. Job and the prophets weren't as "religified" (new word) as some people I meet. What do you mean? Jesus was the way to freedom, healing, etc. and never had excuses, not even once, not to heal anybody. He was our example. Paul64 healed every single person on the Island on Malta. Why is it that we look for the few and far between "cracks" in God's goodness and in the lives of New Testament or Old Testament people to define our doubt instead of using the overwhelming evidence for His goodness through Himself, His Son, Jesus Christ, and the New Testament churches' lives. God's will for miracles to and through every believer is so overwhelmingly, yes and amen, it eclipses the few if any negative responses. I truly believe that the body of Christ hasn't gone into the New Testament glory because just like in Numbers 13, we've listened to the doubtful many who disqualified the faith of the couple. Joshua and Caleb brought the report of the Lord whereas the rest of the ten tribes brought a doubtful outlook. What if we are in the wilderness because we haven't moved forward with the Ways of Jesus?

"How will the ministry of the Spirit not be more glorious? For if the ministry of condemnation had glory, the ministry of righteousness exceeds much more in glory. But if the ministry of death, written and engraved on stones, was glorious, so that the children of Israel could not look steadily at the face of Moses because of the glory of his countenance, which glory was passing away." II Corinthians 3:7-9

I promise, I used to do this early before Bible college, but somehow I got off during my journey and started to pray for the things that God told me to pray. Someone convinced me that, although I was seeing some things happen, some experiences with Jesus, I may not have been baptized in the Spirit

---

64 Paul is often cited as the apostle who didn't believe in healing due to his "thorn" in the flesh. Nevertheless, he healed the sick frequently.

like some of the greats. Since I've awakened from that to what I ALREADY HAVE, I have experienced God thousands of times as I obeyed the Words of Jesus. Yes—the New Testament glory! Blind eyes opened, deaf ears opened, cancers healed, stroke victims healed, etc., but it didn't start until I obeyed the Words of Jesus. I just began to take the shot. Just like secret agents are trained to take the shot no matter what the reasoning they have to try to stop them, God has told me to take the shot. See, too many blame the lack of their obedience by the lack of their leading rather than the already revealed will of God through His Son displayed by words and action here on earth.

Why is it that we sit in churches praying for God to protect and provide for us, and save the nations, and then not go and do what the early church did? They turned the known world upside down! Literally, we sing songs and while singing believe that God is somehow saving those around us. I'm going to step on toes now. Many misquote this Scripture from John 12:32, *"If I be lifted up, I will draw all men nigh unto Me."* He wasn't talking about a worship service in a building, that if good enough, would reach the city. No, He was talking about being crucified, explaining He had to die to save the nations. Now, I'm a worshiper, I worship all the time. Our church worship is long. Like, I go for His glory, but this isn't the context of this Scripture and I believe it's consoling the conscience of people in place of the commands of Christ. Too many are thinking worship is the obedience to Christ. People are saying, "We were born to worship God." I disagree. Whoa, whoa, okay, hold on! I know it's tradition to quote that but it's not a Scripture. John 17:3 says, *"And this is eternal life, that they may know You, the only true God, and Jesus Christ whom You have sent." John 17:3 NKJV.* We are made for a relationship with Him. Yes, we worship, but it's to be in relationship with Him. Since we know Him, we must make Him known to others around us. It's just how love works.

JESUS IS GENIUS

Some of the many discoveries of the Bible line up with science. In the Old Testament, God said to wait for the eighth day after a baby's birth before circumcision. I know it sounds random, but it's because God knew that babies' blood didn't produce the enzyme needed for blood clotting until that day. Now He didn't specify that, but He did give a command for that. Fasting! Oh my gosh, look at all the evidence for fasting these days. Intermittent fasting, daily fasting, larger times of fasting. I remember watching the documentary called, "Science of Fasting." It is a science-based documentary by a secular scientist. I was completely fascinated with the breakthrough they were discovering. Who said fasting would bring healing? God, in Isaiah 58 mostly, but the truth is scattered through Scripture. God doesn't just lay out a thesis for us to read, because the benefits of His Word or the "secrets" of His Word are for them that fear Him65 or take Him seriously. Time could fail me to talk about the benefits of lifestyles and choices that the Bible talks about to heal our bodies or preserve them in a scientific way.

Just one of His ways is to make disciples. He said to teach them to observe everything He commanded them. If one person makes three disciples in a year and teaches those disciples to make three disciples, and every year they repeat, in twenty years we would have seen three billion souls discipled. How

---

65 Psalm 25:14

much good have we done in the world as the church in twenty years? We've declined. Why? The majority of believers and their pastors do not support the Jesus we see in the Bible. It shouldn't surprise us that a lesser level produces lesser results.

Why don't we disciple? It would require change. Why don't we heal the sick? It would require us finding God for real revelation. Why don't we cast out demons? It's work! Everything Jesus said required change. I believe this is why the Pharisees and the religious crucified Jesus and why religious people can't stand people breaking through with power in their ministry. It's because they sacrificed so much to get to where they are that change is now an enemy. I believe that's where the body of Christ is; we are wanting God to do what He commanded us to do and then blaming Him for all the chaos. But Jesus works! It's genius.

I see believers all day online correcting governments, ministries, and whoever they can find instead of actually making disciples. What would happen if we used all the energy we use for social media, disagreements, and things in our lives to advance the Kingdom? It would work. It would change nations.

I promise, I worked at a Spirit-filled Bible college. Other than our evangelism professor, hardly anyone believed in evangelism personally. Isn't that a little odd? The very reason the Holy Spirit came was to empower #Every Believer with love, power, and a sound mind to do what Jesus did, everywhere. Nobody seems called to do anything that demands change. How is that? Is it the lack of sovereign calling or maybe doctrines we declare that are divine?

We need to see Christ's Words as God's Word. Jesus said to obey His commandments, not Moses'. Oh mercy, I can hear it, "This man is telling people to break Moses' laws." Nope, but I am saying that Jesus' laws fulfilled all of Moses. I am saying I am a follower of Christ and not Moses. I am saying that Moses worshiped Jesus and here we are contending for Moses when we are in a New Dispensation. The same Ways carry the same fruit. Will you be one of the ones? I am praying for revelation to spring forth and God's power to come upon you!

TRAGEDY IN THE CHURCH

I am really concerned that people come up with doctrines so that they don't have to change. We find people to agree with us. Pastor, preacher, prophet, friend, or whoever— "please tell me that I don't have to do what Jesus said. Tell me it's a gift and not a calling. Tell me it's for some and not for all." I tell you, the generation in Biblical times said, "What shall we do to be saved,"[66] but now they say, "Do we have to do that to be saved?" It's a heart condition. You know we are still in the spiritual Dark Ages in some capacity, when talking about Jesus being for radical people.

---

66 Acts 2:38

5.

JESUS, THE WALKING COVENANT

Jesus was the New Covenant walking around us. He healed the sick, forgave the sinner, cast out demons, made the maimed whole, among other things. He said, *"Freely you receive, Freely give."* (Matthew 10:8). He was the new normal. Most people have missed it, He was the NEW NORMAL. That's what a New Covenant meant. A New Way to expect. A New Way to see and relate to God. Now it's Jesus. He's our Way to see God. He's our Way to receive from God. He's our Way to see God move through us! He's our New Normal. Can you see it? He was what we could expect from God and God through us because of His perfect blood shed to clear on our account.

We can be waiting for something else other than Jesus. Look, whether you believe this book to be true or not, you are reading this book, because there is part of you that believes there is more. There is part of you that isn't satisfied. Inherently, no matter the religious reasons we have inside of us for not having more, we know there is more. Jesus, is this more!

In the context of John 14, Jesus was revealing to His disciples who was BEHIND all of the healings, miracles, forgiveness, etc. He knew, just like us, they were waiting for something else, other than Jesus, to be the final revelation and unfolding of the

Father and His Will for us. We are waiting for the right revelation, the right impartation, we are waiting for SOMETHING. We don't know what and frankly, neither did they.

Jesus says to His disciples, "If you had known Me, you would have known My Father also; from now on you know Him, and have seen Him." John 14:7. What was He saying? The Father was revealing Himself through Christ. We just haven't taken Him seriously.

The works through Him, the Words through Him, the forgiveness of adulteress women through Him, had all been the Father revealing Himself to them. At that point, I wish I would have been like, "YES!!!!!, You are the secret to knowing God and His will for life!!" But Philip's response was this: *"Philip said to Him, 'Lord, show us the Father, and it is enough for us.'" John 14:8.* Wow. Philip was basically saying, "Stop playing around Jesus, show us the real Father and we will be happy." The crazy thing is, that's what many of us do when it comes to believing Jesus in our theology, outside of just Him being our Way for forgiveness! God, what's Your will...Jesus. No really God, what's your will for healing? What's your will for discipleship? What's your will for my destiny? So many don't think Jesus is ACTUALLY the revealing of every will of God for us.

Wow, imagine, if the disciples who had walked with Jesus had missed this truth bomb, maybe we could be missing this side of Jesus too. Later on in John 14:12, we hear Jesus saying, "If you believe in Me, these works you shall do and even greater, because I go to the Father." Jesus was SAYING, in context, that if we see His life like it was the FATHER REVEALING HIMSELF through Him and not just a neat time period or odd occurrence with Jesus, we would have faith to see the same and even greater miracles once Jesus left. Why? Because we would see the miracles and movement of Jesus like it really was, the revealing of God Himself. His life was the Father communicating His perfect will for every believer from now on. If they could see it wasn't just a one-time show or season, then they could have confidence that this WAS THE WILL of God moving forward for every disciple or believer of Jesus.

There is no more mystery. Jesus revealed who God was more than any prophet or anyone before Him. John 1:18 says, "No one has seen God at any time; the only begotten God who is in the bosom of the Father, He has explained Him." The Greek word for "explained" Him is Strong's G1834 - "exegeomai." One of the used definitions of this word is "UNFOLDED."

Imagine if I folded up useful instructions for an important job and told you to figure the job out only by the words you could read, without unfolding the piece of paper. You might be able to read a few words, but you couldn't intimately understand the instructions could you?

In the Old Testament, the revelation of God was FOLDED. John 3:3 says, "Unless you are born again, you cannot SEE the Kingdom of heaven." This passage means UNDERSTANDING the Kingdom. In the Old Testament, they weren't born again so they couldn't UNDERSTAND God properly. He was folded in a mystery.

Even in Galatians, until Christ came, the people were under a law, because they weren't born again. It's almost like when you aren't born again, you don't understand the things of God like a young child doesn't understand life. I have three children. They are thirteen, eleven, and nine years of age. They understand a lot more now than when they were two, because no matter how much I told them WHY they shouldn't do things, when they were two, they would still try. Why? Their understanding wasn't open. I had to use a "law" of sorts to hold them back from doing dangerous things. For instance, I would tell my kids not to go near the road and explain over and over what repercussions might happen if they did, but they didn't listen until a "law" was in place. The "law" for my kids was discipline, but the law for the Israelites was the actual Law.

"But before faith came, we were kept in custody under the law, being shut up to the faith which was later to be revealed. Therefore the Law has become our tutor to lead us to Christ, so that we may be justified by faith. But now that faith has come, we are no longer under a tutor." Galatians 3:23-25

The same is still true today. Why do we have laws? Because everyone is like a child, because we can't be Biblically righteous or know God until we are born again. From a young age we don't have to teach kids to do what's wrong, but what's right. They NATURALLY do what's wrong. The laws of every country are only there because hearts are evil, and even in old age, people don't have understanding of God or His ways so that's why the law was invented through the Jews. They will kill when not accountable, steal when they can, or destroy whenever they can't be found out. The Bible says, "The heart is deceitful above all things, And desperately wicked; Who can know it?" Jeremiah 17:9 NKJV. So the law, although hard to grasp, was necessary. God was still a gentle giant, He just needed a way to hold wickedness back until Christ came.

In the same way, Jesus unfolded God to us by the Way of His life. He was unfolding God and His Will by preaching the Gospel, casting out demons, healing those who were broken hearted, forgiving those who were caught in sin, healing the sick, and making disciples. Jesus was the New Covenant, not only for salvation, but for every way for us to follow.

INTENT IS EVERYTHING

God's intent is seen at the beginning of creation. There was no sickness or disease; it was perfect. God made everything good and blessed it, and then we came along.

"For the creation was subjected to futility, not willingly, but because of Him who subjected it in hope; because the creation itself also will be delivered from the bondage of corruption into the glorious liberty of the children of God." Romans 8:20-21

I was visiting a friend's house and their dog had hurt its leg. I know—"a dog? Really?" Yup. I held its leg and this compassionate voice from heaven spoke to me and said, "This isn't what I intended creation to be under." If God has compassion for a dog, I know He has more compassion and INTENT for our healing. His plan for humankind and the world was for a healthy life. His intent is seen at the cross; *"But He was wounded **for our transgressions**, He was bruised **for our iniquities**; The chastisement **for our peace** was upon Him, And **by His stripes** we are healed." Isaiah 53:5 (emphasis mine). "But God demonstrates His own love toward us, in that while we were still sinners, Christ died for us." Romans 5:8.* This is HOW we know God's love for us, that while we were sinners, Christ died. This is the best part of Jesus, the innocent died for us, the guilty. The world was perfect and this is why things shifted; we sinned. Our sins separated us from God, His Goodness, and blessing, both temporarily and eternally.

THE CONSEQUENCE AND SALVATION FOR SIN

"It's your sins that have cut you off from God. Because of your sins, he has turned away and will not listen anymore." Isaiah 59:2 NLT

The curse was the punishment for sins we would commit. Here is a list of punishments that would happen as a result of our sin. Remember, we sinned, and God had to wage a war to KEEP sin at bay UNTIL Jesus would make a final offering, once and for all, for our sins. After this Scripture, it gets good.

"Now it shall come to pass, if you diligently obey the voice of the Lord your God, to observe carefully all His commandments which I command you today, that the Lord your God will set you high above all nations of the earth. And all these blessings shall come upon you and overtake you, because you obey the voice of the Lord your God: But it shall come to pass, if you do not obey the voice of the Lord your God, to observe carefully all His commandments and His statutes which I command you today, that all these curses will come upon you and overtake you: Cursed shall be the fruit of your body and the produce of your land, the increase of your cattle and the offspring of your flocks. The Lord will make the plague cling to you until He has consumed you from the land which you are going to possess. The Lord will strike you with consumption, with fever, with inflammation, with severe burning fever, with the sword,

with scorching, and with mildew; they shall pursue you until you perish. And your heavens which are over your head shall be bronze, and the earth which is under you shall be iron. The Lord will strike you with the boils of Egypt, with tumors, with the scab, and with the itch, from which you cannot be healed. Moreover all these curses shall come upon you and pursue and overtake you, until you are destroyed, because you did not obey the voice of the Lord your God, to keep His commandments and His statutes which He commanded you. Then the Lord will bring upon you and your descendants extraordinary plagues—great and prolonged plagues—and serious and prolonged illnesses. Moreover He will bring back on you all the diseases of Egypt, of which you were afraid, and they shall cling to you. Also every sickness and every plague, which is not written in this Book of the Law, will the Lord bring upon you until you are destroyed. And among those nations you shall find no rest, nor shall the sole of your foot have a resting place; but there the Lord will give you a trembling heart, failing eyes, and anguish of soul." Deuteronomy 28:1-2, 15, 18, 21-23, 27, 45, 59-61, 65

The Bible says, «*The wages of our sin was death.*" Romans 6:23. Because we sinned or sin, our bodies were subject to the curse(s) given for our sin, but here comes the BEST NEWS IN THE UNIVERSE:

"Christ has redeemed us from the curse of the law, having become a curse for us (for it is written, "Cursed is everyone who hangs on a tree"), that the blessing of Abraham might come upon the Gentiles in Christ Jesus, that we might receive the promise of the Spirit through faith." Galatians 3:13-14

THE BRONZE SERPENT

When He died, He literally became the whipping post for what we deserved. God placed everything we deserved on Him at the cross in order that we could be free from the curse of sin, when we placed our faith in Christ. That means every curse written above was put on Jesus, in our place, so that when we believed we could be healed. Here is the Biblical and symbolic reference for the very transaction previously discussed.

"Then they journeyed from Mount Hor by the Way of the Red Sea, to go around the land of Edom; and the soul of the people became very discouraged on the way. And the people spoke against God and against Moses: 'Why have you brought us up out of Egypt to die in the wilderness? For there is no food and no water, and our soul loathes this worthless bread.' So the Lord sent fiery serpents among the people, and they bit the people; and many of the people of Israel died. Therefore the people came to Moses, and said, 'We have sinned, for we have spoken against the Lord and against you; pray to the Lord that He take away the serpents from us.' So Moses prayed for the people. So Moses made a bronze serpent and put it on the flag pole; and it came about, that if a serpent bit someone, and he looked at the bronze serpent, he lived. Then the Lord said to Moses, 'Make a fiery serpent, and put it on a flagpole; and it shall come about, that everyone who is bitten, and looks at it, will live.'"Numbers 21:1-9

"So that everyone who believes will have eternal life in Him. And just as Moses lifted up the serpent in the wilderness, so must the Son of Man be lifted up." John 3:14-15

Jesus literally bore our curse so that we could have the blessing. He was forsaken so that we could call Him Immanuel. Sin was the only reason bad things came into this world and when Jesus died, that separation from God and all He had for you was ripped apart. You are now forgiven and given the same access Jesus was given.

This is why communion is so powerful. It is literally the appropriation of what Christ took away from us. Sickness, depression, poverty thinking, divorce, disease and the rest are just punishments for our sin. We can renounce those things while we take communion. Jesus literally became the curse so that we could be blessed...not have our sins charged against us. By the way, sin is the only reason there was any sickness, separation, or curses in this world. Since Jesus blood has taken SIN AWAY from our lives, these things have no right to stay in our lives. Getting healed and staying healed is more about us appropriating what Christ has already done to keep our boundaries safe than it does Him protecting us sovereignly. Our whole covenant is by faith so we must appropriate everything He's done for us by faith.

The grace of Jesus, blood of Jesus, the love of Jesus, and identity of sons and daughters is amazing. The tragedy of this day is that they are used to replace obedience. Those revelations were needed. Many were tapping out due to condemnation and shame. Even this revelation of Jesus the Way provides much more access to all of His blessings! The issue is that the body of Christ has USED that message to primarily get the blessings from heaven and to defend their lives of not obeying.

We have completely misunderstood grace, the blood, love, and the identity of Christ if it has led us to be entitled to His promises but dismissed from obedience. I believe that this book is a message in the body of Christ. God is trying to awaken #Every Believer to follow Christ again. Where are our relationships with God when we want the benefits but not the sacrifice? Have we heard the true Gospel of Jesus? I'm concerned we've entered into the season where we have "itching ears" and love the benefits but deny the change. Jesus said, *"Why do they call me 'Lord Lord,' and don't do what I say?" Luke 6:46.*

"Holding to a form of godliness although they have denied its power; avoid such people as these." 2 Timothy 3:5

"And they will turn their ears away from the truth and will turn aside to myths. For the time will come when they will not tolerate sound doctrine; but wanting to have their ears tickled, they will accumulate for themselves teachers in accordance with their own desires." 2 Timothy 4:3-4

I believe if you are reading this book you are hungry for more, and this is the more. Jesus is the Way and God is flipping the script. If you are hungry for more and willing to change, then He will have it easy bringing breakthroughs your way. For the most part, I truly believe that most of our hang ups lie in a wrong religious interpretation of Scripture. I pray this next chapter will bring revelation of God's power and intent into your situation and the Spirit of God will cause you to soar more than you could have ever imagined! I'm praying God's Spirit would roar in and through you while you read!

6.

IF RELIGION CAN'T KILL US, IT CONFORMS US

I was dazed and confused. I had been walking with Jesus and having powerful times, fasting, participating in leadership with a teen ministry, preaching the Gospel, praying for the sick, casting out demons, and giving food to the homeless—when suddenly, I moved to almost nothing. What happened? I began to read books of great men of God, who moved in more power than I did. I began to compare my experiences with others. I didn't take the forewarning of Paul, *"For we dare not class ourselves or compare ourselves with those who commend themselves. But they, measuring themselves by themselves, and comparing themselves among themselves, are not wise." 2 Corinthians 10:12 NKJV.* It was just a religious false humility that came on me. I started to say I wasn't baptized in the Holy Spirit. I went to Bible college to find God like some of these generals did. All the while, I was looking for the "true" baptism in the Holy Spirit, I stopped praying for the sick, preaching the Gospel, prayer walking, etc. I even started to think I wasn't saved for a small season. It was getting dark, real dark. I was being oppressed and had no joy whatsoever. I praise God for pastors. I was at Bible college and I asked one of my professors about what I was going through.

He totally pulled me out by showing me it wasn't God, and there was almost an overnight change. I had joy—I was waiting for something I already had but had stopped using. I was growing, but I just listened to the wrong influences to stop everything, until I had an encounter like these people. Comparison will kill you through guilt or pride; either way, it wants to take the Jesus that is already walking in us, out. It was okay to use examples of believers who have gone before us as inspiration, growth, and support to walk like Christ, but not for comparison to their conversion stories or baptism in the Holy Spirit encounters. Whew! Religion, whether comparison, legalism, false grace, or anything that isn't from Jesus will always try to take us out. Since that time in my life, I've seen thousands of instantaneous healings, fruitfulness with prophecy and words of knowledge, boldness like never before, and just a love walk with Christ that is full of Joy. Jesus truly is the Way to live!

I believe that religion, or the spirit of religion, is the biggest killer or restriction to worldwide salvation and revival. I've seen sinners in false religions find Christ, non-Spirit filled believers get the Holy Spirit, and Spirit-filled believers become empowered and healed by the Holy Spirit after training. Religion always stops people from entering the doorway to Christ. Whether in salvation, healing, power, deliverance, direction, and fulfillment, religion blocks us from what Christ has paid for us to receive. Either way, If we are honest, there are parts of it that hold us back. It's the parts of us that like the praise of man and not the praise of God. That part of us likes praise for what we do and not for what God asks us to do. It's the thought that makes our weaknesses seem like a holy calling. Religion, that is, not from God, is one of the most dangerous things we can have.

The first time religion tried to kill Jesus, He rose again and the message multiplied. I'm sure the devil took notes. When righteous people are martyred, it's a seed for revival or salvation for multiplication. Jesus even said, "Unless a seed falls to the ground."[67] Now it's not as if that's the goal, but I believe the enemy couldn't kill the Way, so he tried to pacify it. Just think, it only took around 250 years to turn the known world upside down, when death was the threat. But when religion started to be implemented by Constantine, the church died; that was about 1200 years ago. Mixture is worse than death threats. Mixture is ADDING worldly thinking into God's Way and then calling it holy. It killed us. It's time for us to awaken to the naked truth of the Lord Jesus Christ!

"What is the will of the Lord?" I remember sitting with one of my members who had back pain. We were discussing how to know the will of God. *"It may be or it may not be the will of God,"* he said. I told him that in order to have faith, we must have the revelation of God's will or Word indefinitely. He said, *"How can anyone know the will of the Lord absolutely?"* I answered, "We only know the will of the Lord by His Word." Romans 10:17 (NASB) says, "So faith comes from hearing, and hearing by the word of Christ." That means, He revealed His will to men who spoke it or wrote it or revealed it to us by His Spirit. He got it! *"Oh, God's will is known by His Word,"* he said. As soon as he said these words, we felt the presence of God, and he said 50% of his back pain went away without praying! The right version of who Jesus is, brings in the right blessing.

---

67 John 12:24

RELIGION IS THE PROBLEM

"Making the word of God of no effect through your tradition which you have handed down. And many such things you do."
Mark 7:13

There's an old story told about traditions of men. It goes something like this:

> "A very poor holy man lived in a remote part of China. Every day before his time of meditation in order to show his devotion, he put a dish of butter up on the window sill as an offering to God, since food was so scarce. One day his cat came in and ate the butter. To remedy this, he began tying the cat to the bedpost each day before the quiet time. This man was so revered for his piety that others joined him as disciples and worshiped as he did. Generations later, long after the holy man was dead, his followers placed an offering of butter on the window sill during their time of prayer and meditation. Furthermore, each one bought a cat and tied it to the bedpost."

This is *Webster's* definition of *tradition:* "an inherited, established, or customary pattern of thought, action, or behavior."

Tradition is meant to be repetitive. It's something enjoyable that has sentimental value. Since we figured out something we like, that we benefit from, let us make it a normal expectation. Some traditions are amazing. The problem with some traditions is that they are in direct contradiction to what was meant by God to be powerful, and they are reduced to just good. Religious traditions make us feel special about what we do. Many times, they are not Biblical but treated holy. The problem with religious traditions is that they limit us from experiencing all that God has meant for us. Jesus said they make the power of God of no effect.[68]

Jesus was against religious traditions, because He knew the power they had to stop people from salvation and the benefits of salvation. You can hear His aggression when He's talking to the religious elites of that day; "But woe to you, scribes and Pharisees, hypocrites, because you shut the kingdom of heaven in front of people; for you do not enter it." Matthew 23:13. Jesus saw the ways of the Pharisees to be dangerous enough to stop salvation. If the Master was that convinced we must be awakened to allow the Holy Spirit to search our hearts and begin to unwrap the power of God that's in every believer that has been baptized with the power of the Holy Spirit.

SOMETIMES WHAT SEEMS TO BE GOOD, TAKES OUT GOD

Religion makes things holy that were never said by God! It is the biggest infiltrator that limits the power of God. It seems good but it never brings God. So many people say God can do anything or nothing can stop God but God said the "traditions of man make the power of God of no effect."

What does it really matter? Does knowing the truth really make that big of a deal? If it's true, shouldn't it just happen? These are questions I get when talking about healing, deliverance, and Jesus being the Way to all of it. It's a BIG DEAL how we believe. It's the governor of what comes in our lives and what flows out of us!

---

68 Mark 7:13

Most of Christendom believe that Jesus is the only Way to salvation. That's an accepted foundation. I mean, people will fight over it because it's contingent on salvation in modern Christendom. (In case anyone has any concerns, I strictly believe Jesus to be the only Way to salvation as well.)

Why does it matter if I don't believe exactly like the Bible? Why are you so set on believing a certain Way about healing? Is this another Word of Faith book? Shouldn't it just happen IF IT'S TRUE? No. Just because Jesus has died on the cross and IS THE SAVIOR of the world, it doesn't automatically make everyone saved or come to know Him. Just because something is available it doesn't mean it automatically happens. It has to be the right version, an actual revelation on a personal level. When people just hear someone's opinion or another version, it can stop the power of God. Their lack of revelation of the right Jesus, of the Gospel saving power of Jesus, is keeping them from salvation.

For instance, I meet many Muslims who believe in a form of Jesus, but not THE Jesus most Christians believe in. Does it do them any good? NO. It's almost worse than if they hadn't heard Him at all. Why? Because it's false hope that gives a form of comfort. This false hope leaves them hanging from the true experience, yet accepted in a culture as the way to follow.

As believers, we believe this not for doctrinal purposes or safety purposes only, but for a tangible reality. The right Gospel produces the right results. They aren't born again. They don't get born again, unless they relate to Christ as the Messiah instead of only one of the prophets. So yes, we say Jesus is the

Only Way for doctrinal purity and also for the literal power of the Gospel like Paul states in Romans.

"For I am not ashamed of the gospel, for it is the power of God for salvation to everyone who believes, to the Jew first and also to the Greek." Romans 1:16 NKJV

I propose that, in the same way a Muslim is blocked from the saving grace because of his wrong beliefs of Christ, so are many Christians blocked from the New Testament power, promises, possibilities, and life we see in the Bible and read in early church history records.

In the same manner, the right version of the Gospel, who Jesus was, is, and will be is the foundation of us receiving and walking in anything He portrayed. Could it be possible that some people believe in a different Jesus than the Bible, when it comes to healing, but think they should get the same results as if they had the right version? Could it be possible that some are proclaiming a New Testament reality but with a man made interpretation, thus limiting their experience? Could it be possible that we have a New Testament proclamation but not experience? I believe we are on the brink of an every believer revival. Everyone is waking up to the power of God that He's always intended!

RELIGION IS SECRETLY OKAY WITH NOT HAVING GOD IN ITS CAMP.

"Now there was a man of the Pharisees, named Nicodemus, a ruler of the Jews; this man came to Jesus at night and said to Him, 'Rabbi, we know that You have come from God as a teacher; for no one can do these signs that You do unless God is with him.'" John 3:1-2

123

The Pharisees knew that Jesus was the Christ but falsely accused him. What does that have to do with me? The temptation of religion is to hold to our ways more than to Christ's ways because there are leaders who support it. I am totally against a jaded mindset towards the church. Although I am attacking religion, I am completely for the church, for discipleship, for true pastors, apostles, and five-fold ministry, it's just supposed to be more powerful.

Imagine—sorcerers or magistrates came to celebrate the Christ, but the religious were nowhere near. Just think, sinners would love Christ, but the religious rejected Christ openly. Wow, a demon possessed girl could recognize that Paul was a man of God more than all the religious elect put together. I'm reminded of a book[69] about William Branham I read. Some spiritualists saw the call of God on him before any religious people. Later, when he was moving in visions and miracles, pastors tried to persuade him he was hearing from the devil. He literally prayed for God to take away these encounters because He believed their advice. God had to visit him to set him straight that he was hearing from God and not demons. Lord awaken our heart to the blinders religion puts on us! We must come to grips that just because we have a FORM of godliness, it does not mean we are with the Savior. It's a scary place where most believers are okay with an experience that doesn't include God. I mean, we would rather have that which is familiar than that which is Godly.

Meetings with no presence of God, no sick being healed, no demons coming out, no love, no repentance, are lacking. Most are triggered by what the media is saying and not obeying what Christ has already said and is still speaking. This is how

69 *Supernatural: The Life of William Branham: Volumes 1-5*

dangerous a religious mindset is. We as a society are like slowly cooked frogs to what is really going on. Yes, we were born into it so no, there isn't condemnation or a need for shame, but there is a need for an awakening!

RELIGION BITES!

My own church was seeing a reformation. Healings and miracles were taking place, but the religious were getting upset. We were loving the lost, seeing so many healings, speaking words of knowledge, and having true discipleship. STILL people were mad. A part of the church split, because they believed a pastor shouldn't be so evangelistic or into healing. Religion, no matter how we cut it, is not only blind to the real Christ, but wants to kill Him!

Religion hates the truth so much that it will try to kill Truth itself. In John 3:12, Nicodemus told Jesus that they knew He was the Christ. I may offend some people, but I believe that religion stops God more than sin itself. Jesus sat with the sinners, not with the religious! Why? Religion is all about glorifying the acts of man, not the acts of God! Religion gets praised for things in the flesh more than things actually directed by God Himself. It says in John 12:43, *"For they loved the praise of men more than the praise of God."* They killed Jesus because He was stealing the show. Now personally, He was just following the Father, as do many and as we were in our own church, but the religious won't have it.

Mark 12:7 "But those vinedressers said among themselves, 'This is the heir. Come, let us kill him, and the inheritance will be ours.'"

Reading this Scripture above, there wasn't one good intention. There is no good intention. Although they told everyone their intent was pure, their hidden agenda was to steal His glory. He was taking their game. Even today, the only people that most of contemporary Christianity are against are those being used in the supernatural. Just watch, religion looks like it's fighting for truth but it's fighting for their territory. I know we are attached to people and would never like to think of them like this, but that same spirit of religion is alive today, still trying to take Jesus out.

Why do I say this? Because once you start operating like Jesus, being limitless like Jesus, some people may not join you or even oppose you. Your church may even resist you. Maybe even family may come against you. Jesus warned us that even our families would come against us. Those who are closest to us, who would love to support us, actually come against us and even ridicule us. Even David in 1 Samuel 17, who was doing the Lord's work, was ridiculed by his own brother like he was doing something evil. It's okay; we are not called to convince the haters. Jesus wouldn't perform signs for His haters, the religious. All day long He did signs for the lost people of Israel and His disciples, but not those who were just trying to prove Him wrong. To really be used by God, you must get to the point of being okay with people who will not understand you, misquote you, or just plainly lie about you.

WE ARE IN NEED OF REFORMATION!

Paul says this, *"And my message and my preaching were not in persuasive words of wisdom, but in demonstration of the Spirit and of power,"* *1 Corinthians 2:4.* I have a degree in Biblical theology but the degree itself never healed anyone. It never cast demons out or saved anyone. YES, it is of utmost importance to know hermeneutics, but not at the expense of power. As the body of Christ, we are too famous in polarizing one side of only doctrine or the other side of only Spirit rather than FOLLOWING the Biblical precedent that Jesus, Paul, and the New Testament believers followed.

We are in need of those who aren't sworn to the familiar but see what God is saying for the future. There is still a reformation happening from the Dark Ages. The Dark Ages? Yes. We refer to this time as the ages where religion started to creep into the church. It started to affect the church in early 300 AD. The emergence from the Dark Ages started with Martin Luther in the 1500's with his 95 theses. Luther was in law school, but dropped out and went into a monastery to fulfill a vow he made to God during a thunderstorm in 1505. After getting his doctorate, he received knowledge that priests were taking indulgences (money) to take away people's sins. He posted these 95 theses on a castle church in Wittenburg, Germany, in disagreement with this and many other wrong doctrines of the church. From that time, the grip that religion had on the church has started to be dismantled. John Wesley, George Whitfield, Charles Spurgeon, Charles Finney, Evan Roberts, William Seymour, Charles Parham, T.L. Osborn, Billy Graham, and more are men that God has used to bring His already-revealed will back into practice. We are STILL undoing some of that religion to which we are accustomed.

Wait, wait! This cannot just be history or another story. What did Martin Luther have to gain? Think of it. The whole church was against him in this. Change, when the whole group is deceived, is never fun. He wasn't getting followers on Facebook or Twitter, but rather death threats that weren't empty threats. He literally counted that his life was worth his challenging the system. Why? Because of the people. One of the most famous quotes whose author is debated is this: *"The only thing necessary for the triumph of evil is for good men to do nothing."* He wasn't against the church, just the pagan traditions that were deceiving people and leading them away from true faith in Jesus Christ.

This is outlandish in its reality, but I truly believe that the body of Christ wants to see the revivals, miracles, and movements that happened through great men of God. However, we don't want to believe what they believed or do what they did. This is religion at its root. The works of Jesus are possible but it requires us to come to the end of what traditions have meant to us in order to really grasp onto the power of the Lord Jesus.

THE CHURCH IS AT A LESS-THAN-MOSAIC REALITY

Just think, the church right now is in less-than-Mosaic format. Israel was all about Israel, their needs, their prosperity, their families, etc., and that was their covenant! But it isn't ours! The current church is doped up on a needs-based Gospel that doesn't produce many disciples—just needy people. The Bible says to seek first the Kingdom of God and all things will be added, but we have taught people to seek God first SO all these things will be added, and the seeking first isn't Christ first, it's church first. What? Yes, I said earlier that it was less than a Mosaic covenant. We are gathering mostly as a form of obedience so that our lives will go well. We are hoping for our families to do well in school, society, financially, and in our country, for these things to prosper us more than the Kingdom of God. Most believers are just trying to survive in life and not actually activated in following Jesus or putting the kingdom of God first, which He actually intended.

Imagine, we are settling to be beggars toward God instead of partners with Him! He always intended for us to be co-laborers[70] with Him and not just recipients. But why isn't this being preached? Because for the most part, the religious are receiving an inheritance from a religious Gospel. No need to be brash but I believe if most pastors, priests, and believers were honest, God's been calling us to the harvest; He's been calling us to change to match the New Testament example. I'm praying for every limitation that has tried to stop you to be removed, and that the power and love of the Spirit of Jesus would fill you!

---

70 1 Corinthians 3:9

7.

WHERE'S THE POWER?

This was my first time going outside the church with the purpose of healing the sick or expecting a power encounter in 13 years. I remember walking up to my first potential person needing prayer. I had really been like the lady with the issue of blood to talk to myself. I kept saying to myself, "They are going to be healed, they are going to be healed," as I walked up. I introduced myself like this, "Hey, my name is Greg Gervais, WE (I was by myself) are ministers who pray for people and see them healed. Do you have any pain in your body right now? Anything that is regularly hurting?" She said she did! Woohoo—at least I found a proper prospect. Joy surged through my heart. This may be the one...her wrist had been hurting for some time. So I said, "Do you want that to go away?" She answered, "Of course." I grabbed her wrist and prayed, "In Jesus' name, pain go! Jesus, Your love is amazing for her, thank You for healing this wrist." I asked her if she was feeling anything. She replied that she felt some tingling in her wrist. I was ecstatic. I asked her to move it around. She did and said there was no pain. I was so surprised she was healed. I asked her again if it was 100% gone; she said there was no pain! I said, "This is to show you that Jesus really loves you." And I left. This was a breakthrough encounter that has led to thousands more!!!

At five years old, I gave my life to Christ with my mom in our car. I think I was actually saved. I remember telling people about Jesus afterwards. At some age in kids ministry, the kids pastor tried to get us filled with the Holy Spirit by praying for us and then having us repeat similar syllables, but I never sensed power coming in me. I never disregarded the Holy Spirit, but just moved on.

I was 16 and starting to awaken to the promptings of the Holy Spirit to personally follow Christ. I got baptized in water and started to seek God for His power. I started to look for God in the church, go to youth ministry, and explore my options. Not finding a whole lot of Jesus, I looked for books. I heard more and more of the power of the Holy Spirit by the odd pastor visiting our church or just randomly on television. At some point, I picked up the book *Good Morning, Holy Spirit* by Benny Hinn. Wow! The Holy Spirit in person was possible! I devoured the book within days (for 16, that's pretty hungry). I finished the book and thought, "I want this."

It seemed to start in the morning with Benny Hinn, so I started off saying, "Good Morning, Holy Spirit," every morning. I would wait for "IT" but nothing happened. After a while of not really sensing anything during these trials, I moved onto afternoons and evenings. Good Afternoon, Holy Spirit; Good Evening, Holy Spirit—and not seeing what the book seems to invite its readers to experience, I was like, "Good Night, Holy Spirit."

I was frustrated and turned to my own ways. I started to mix with the wrong crowd and do what they did until I was about twenty years old. I thank God He never let me go too far or get lost, considering how many seemed to get lost. I wasn't having an ear for God and although I was at my worst, God kept pursuing me more than any other time in my whole life. I'd be drinking and feeling the pull of the Holy Spirit. It was almost like a tapping on my shoulder by God—as if He would say, "You know this isn't for you." But, in my stupidity, I disregarded His attempts. I was now having fun.

God took it to the next level, when I broke my wrist, lost my job, went into debt, and other things started to go wrong in my life. I could sense the Lord just waiting by saying, "When will you return?" I calculated that my life mishaps were like a Jonah call over my life; finally, I gave into the pullings of the Holy Spirit on my heart and started going to numerous places looking for Jesus again.

I had a friend who was bringing me to different services where young Catholic priests were laying hands on people and seeing them healed, and some would fall on the ground too. I was taken aback, "Catholics and healing"...I started to get hungry for Jesus again. I would drive to Tehila Monday at First Assembly, where the pullings of the Holy Spirit seemed to drive my choice to follow Christ again, even deeper. My friend who had taken me to some of these Catholic services told me she was going to Boise, Idaho, to miracle services with one of the churches we were attending. She invited me to go with her. I honestly thought, Jesus, and a girl—this sounds great!

So I paid the fee for the trip and the hotel to go to this miracle service. It was two days prior to going and she canceled on me. Half my reasoning to go was taken away, but God knew what He was doing. I sensed a deeper call in spite of the sixteen hours in a greyhound bus on a winding road for much of the way from

Lethbridge, Alberta, to Boise, Idaho. I remember an older gentleman having some issues with his body so he couldn't walk properly. Every corner was like a pinball machine. He would bump into everyone on the way to the restroom and then on the way back to his seat.

Getting to this service was something I had never experienced. Thousands of people lined up for this miracle service. Every night of the conference I was like, "Let him see me, Lord." Although there were 20,000 people there, I thought I had a chance. It was the last night of the conference; two nights had passed, and no one saw me in this crowd—but I was still hungry. I had offered to pray for people during this weekend, and a boy who was deaf started hearing under the presence of God in that room. The last night he called for everyone that was nineteen and under to come up to the front. I was twenty years old, had helped usher during the weekend, and watched everyone get healed and ministered to. At this point, I was so hungry for a touch from God, I left my post of ushering to go to the front to find Jesus.

Although I hurried up to the front, there were still about a thousand young people in front of me. About seven rows of teens were across the whole floor of the stadium. The leader told us to lift our hands up while he prayed and then he shouted, "Fire!" Boom—all seven rows in front of me fell to the ground with this impartation of the Holy Spirit. I was upset again. "God, here am I!" Why hadn't I fallen or gotten this fire? But he saw me and another guy who hadn't fallen and called us onto the stage. As I stood there waiting with my hands up, I felt God coming toward me. Wow, I had never experienced power like this. He was walking toward me and started to say, "fire," but all I heard was the "fi" in word fire, and I was knocked to the floor. I don't know if he touched me or not, but I was down. This heavy blanket of God's presence was on me. Power had hit me! Although I was having this experience, I opened my eyes because of the noise on the stage; the security team and ushers were pulling people off the stage, so I told myself to get up. I started to get up and he saw me again. He said, "fire," but this time I didn't fall, so he then put his hand on my head, said it again, and I was down. I stayed there this time. I just figured God wanted me to stay down.

Wave after wave of God's glory was on me. I had never felt this my whole life. What was really happening? I had vision after vision pass through my mind of the future. It was like an open heaven to God's voice over my life. My heart had been replaced and I had been changed forever.

I got up from that encounter and went back home. There was so much going on inside of me. I started reading my Bible hours a day, worshiping hours a day, prayer walking, praying for sick people, and sharing my faith. Something had happened to me at that meeting. After the excitement settled, this deep sense of calling came to my soul, "Where's God in the church?" I wasn't jaded, just challenged by God to bring His power back to the church.

The crazy significance of this power encounter was that it was at a Benny Hinn conference. What??? Remember the book I read, *Good Morning, Holy Spirit*, by Benny Hinn? Yup. God is good, because by that time I had almost forgotten about the book and even the significance of this power encounter. The same author that had frustrated me earlier when I was 16 was used by God to give me the Holy Spirit without me having any logical part in it.

Fast forward ten years. I went to Bible college, got (tripped up) in religious thinking, worked full time for a church, and planted a church. By then I was a little weighed down by some of the traditional ministers I had served under and almost forgot my quest to see God's power in real time, in the church. Not to be cliche, but it was like it was just yesterday. I was in a fasting and prayer time with Jesus and He spoke to me vividly. He said, "You know you're a senior pastor, right?" I responded perhaps how the disciples did when Jesus said, "Someone touched me." I said, "Well, of course." He said, "I want you to go heal the sick again, and this time it will work." Wow! Really, there was a season I prayed for the sick, some were healed, most were not. I had many encounters in His presence but the years of serving others' visions seemed to cancel the healing part. From this encounter, I had all the confidence in the world. I spent a lot of time with Jesus BEFORE I started to go, just to get my mind detached from religion again. I believed that I already had the power. The Holy Spirit came upon me to give me power, so I just had to walk like I really believed. I started to approach people to see if they had pain in their body, and boom—healing after healing took place. This was an easy doorway to share the Gospel of Jesus. It works! I did have the power of the Holy Spirit! This was ten years ago. Since then, we have seen thousands of people healed, deliverances, salvations, encounters, disciples produced, and more since then. Throughout all of this, God has developed in me an awakening for people in the body of Christ. Everything in this book has been the process that God has shown me to awaken people one by one in walking in His power and being used by

Him greatly. When we teach these principles, people receive impartation or ability to do the works of Jesus. I pray you would encounter the same Holy Spirit and be equipped to walk like Jesus did as you read this. I'm praying for you to receive power!

EMBARRASSED

I remember being on a church drama team when I was seventeen, a time when I was completely shy about my faith. I had grown up in church but was still timid. I thought I had A JESUS, but was not full at all of the Holy Spirit. One time, we were doing an event and we were supposed to be human signs toward our drama in the park. I was freaked out. Oh man, what if my friends see me? So I blocked or turned away my face the whole outreach so nobody could see me. I had no boldness whatsoever. I don't think this type of situation, even with adults, is a limited reaction, I believe this is the state of the church. The church is embarrassed. Statistics show that 98% of the church do not share their faith on a regular basis. In this chapter, I believe you will receive insight on why there is a lack of boldness with believers in the world.

I was the evangelism pastor for a local church in Olive Branch, Mississippi. We were successfully able to teach people how to evangelize, and we would regularly go door to door and do outreaches in many places. The strategy was based on the *Way of the Master* by Ray Comfort as well as D. James Kennedy's Evangelism *Explosion*. These books, even today, are great resources and can work to bring the Gospel. However, they are intimidating and a little confrontational. There was still something lacking. This was the power of the Holy Spirit. The Gospel is so powerful in itself. These methods are awesome, and I totally support them, but we can't stop there. The Bible presents a much more powerful version of being a witness.

Why was the New Testament church so bold? Because they had received power. What? God backed them up. Now, we have a culture of religious tradition that doesn't support a tangible God backing us up so, of course, there is no boldness. Some of this power dwindling has to do with a misunderstanding about tongues in a teaching of no power and even a misunderstanding of the role of tongues. Many will say they speak in tongues and think that is the complete Baptism of the Holy Spirit, but the power was that which changed them into other men and women. Look at Peter, he would deny Christ in front of a servant girl and then be able to die upside down on a cross. What changed? The Baptism of the Holy Spirit. The New Testament church was bold because they had power. They knew God was with them and would back them up. He did too! They turned the known world upside down by preaching the Gospel. Guess what, due to fear and being embarrassed, the current church doesn't share their faith. Why? Well, it could be a few things but transactionally, if we look at the New Testament, it's because they don't have power.

Here's what's happened. We had a great Azusa Street Revival that spread all over the world with power. Charles Parham and William Seymour were the first of many revivalists. One of the biggest awakenings we have seen in our day was that outpouring. The problem with anything is, man gets involved and traditions are reborn. We had people making doctrines that, unless you speak in tongues, you aren't saved. This was in response to the Baptists or other denominations saying that tongues were from the devil. You can't make a doctrine that is made out of rejection. There is no Scripture that says that. Yes, they spoke in tongues and prophesied in Acts 2, 8, 10, and 19 upon being filled with the Spirit, but that doesn't say someone isn't saved. Why is this an issue? Well, we have all these supposed Spirit-filled believers that speak in tongues or maybe prophesy and feel like they have made it. As if the goal was tongues. I know I'll step on toes here, but we have a misplaced theology.

You shall receive POWER, when the Holy Spirit comes upon you.[71] Power was the purpose of the Holy Spirit. To do what? To transform us with His power,[72] give us boldness,[73] His love,[74] and purity. But we focus on the tongues. I want to challenge you that 644 million spirit filled believers speak with tongues but don't have or have been changed by power. Power is what was supposed to come upon us when the Holy Spirit came. That power would change us into different people.[75] Look at Samson, when the Spirit of God came upon him, he was a different person. Look at Saul, he received from the prophets and the Holy Spirit changed Him. Look at Peter, changed from the guy who denied Christ to the man who was crucified upside down. Even before I was baptized with the Holy Spirit, I was truly afraid of people, but after I was baptized by the Holy Spirit, immediately I was driven by Him to prayer walk, to pray for the sick, and share the Gospel. What was the difference? Power!

---

71   Acts 1:8 NKJV
72   Luke 24:49; Acts 1:8 NKJV
73   Acts 4:31; 2 Timothy 1:6-7 NKJV
74   Romans 5:5 NKJV
75   1 Samuel 10:6 NKJV

Paul said this to Timothy, *"Therefore I remind you to stir up the gift of God which is in you through the laying on of my hands. For God has not given us a spirit of fear, but of power and of love and of a sound mind." II Timothy 1:6-7.* Paul was saying to stir up the gift of God, which is the Holy Spirit. This action would remedy any spirit of fear he was encountering. But wait, this isn't modern teaching, right? We normally claim, encourage, or correct people with verse 7, but context is everything. Paul was saying that the Baptism in the Holy Spirit he received by the laying on of hands wasn't a spirit of fear. He said furthermore, that it was a Spirit of POWER, LOVE, and a SOUND MIND. That sounds like life change. That sounds like what we've been missing.

THE CHURCH HAS JUST BEEN BELIEVING FOR TONGUES INSTEAD OF POWER.

Are you saying this to say this should have happened to all of us? Yes. Are you saying that if we don't have boldness our baptism in the Holy Spirit was illegitimate? No. I'm saying that the church has missed the whole point of the Holy Spirit. He came to come upon us powerfully; therefore, power would fill even our emotional depravities to where we could share the Gospel and expect power. Jesus said, "You shall receive power,"[76] and "tarry in the city of Jerusalem until you are endued with power from on high."[77] I want you to focus on the fact that he said power, not tongues. Yes, don't tune me out, tongues come, but they weren't the focus. The Holy Spirit came for power, tongues were just an amazing byproduct. I understand how awesome tongues are so

---

76   Acts 1:8 NKJV
77   Luke 24:49 NKJV

this is by no means to belittle the gift of tongues. I fully recognize and use the power of speaking in tongues.

Historically, there was a breakthrough of power when the Azusa street revival came with William Seymour, Charles Parham and others gathered to expect the same Holy Spirit as in the book of Acts. It was so supernatural and powerful. The only thing that sabotages a God thing is when people try to control it. Most denominations that are present today were birthed because of a legitimate movement of God. Still, because of our controlling natures, we put it onto paper and say it's the full counsel of God, and there is nothing more or nothing less that God can highlight from Scripture. It's erroneous to think that a man or a movement has all the revelation of the Scriptures properly. So why not have things we have learned as sound doctrine to continue but not limit others based on our lack of experiences? The pentecostal churches, (now a denomination and not just a movement) began to say that unless you were speaking in tongues, you weren't saved. Even later, in Charismatic movements, unbeknownst to them, because of this, they pushed for people to get tongues primarily instead of power. The focus of every Spirit-filled church began to be tongues. I get it, in Acts 2, 8, 10, 19 there were tongues and/or prophecy to accompany the Baptism of the Holy Spirit, but we are still missing the PURPOSE of the Holy Spirit—that is, POWER. He came to transform us into different creatures. We are to be full of the love of God,[78] full of power to heal the sick and cast out demons,[79] full of boldness to preach the Gospel and stand for righteousness.[80] Isaiah 11 really talks about

---

78 Romans 5:5 NKJV
79 Luke 24:49; Acts 1:8; Mark 16:15-18 NKJV
80 2 Timothy 1:6-7; Acts 4:29-31 NKJV

the seven aspects that we get from the Holy Spirit, or, as other Scriptures call it, the seven Spirits of God. Jesus was anointed with these and has given us this same Holy Spirit to move in the same gifts and strength.

I believe that the reason 98% of believers don't share their faith is because of fear. I understand that for many, the problem would be that they don't believe in the gifts or baptisms of the Holy Spirit, but I talked about that earlier. The 644 million believers who are claiming a pentecostal inheritance they came for tongues. I'm not negating tongues nor limiting the power of tongues; however, I am being Biblical to show that power was the purpose—and not tongues. If we started to believe that the Holy Spirit came for power instead of tongues, we would get power. In Matthew 9:29 Jesus said, "According to your faith, let it be done unto you." If things were supposed to automatically happen without our appropriation of faith, then everyone would be saved, because Jesus is the Savior of the World, but they aren't. As soon as they hear the Gospel or the Word of Christ, faith automatically comes (Romans 10:17). Just like William Seymour believed that the Holy Spirit outpouring was still available and received just that, so do we, if we truly believe the Word.

I will even go as far as to say that this fear has closed down other churches' openness to the gifts of the Holy Spirit. Yes, churches that don't believe or don't allow for His movement are solely responsible in the way they responded, but let me just break it down. Many Spirit-filled believers believe it's so much about tongues that if the pastor doesn't let everyone expound in tongues, they are supposedly limiting God. Hear me—tongues are awesome, but even the services we hold aren't all about tongues happenings, or our full expressions of or responses to His presence; that can get a wee bit weird. I tread lightly on this subject. I will not be legalistic in nature in my own ministry, but we do follow a Biblical outline of tongues according to Paul; we believe the believers who don't follow this heart and mind, when it comes to tongues, are messing it up even for the baptism of the Holy Spirit to spread.

"Therefore, if I do not know the meaning of the language, I shall be a foreigner to him who speaks, and he who speaks will be a foreigner to me. Even so you, since you are zealous for spiritual gifts, let it be for the edification of the church that you seek to excel. Therefore let him who speaks in a tongue pray that he may interpret. For if I pray in a tongue, my spirit prays, but my understanding is unfruitful. yet in the church I would rather speak five words with my understanding, that I may teach others also, than ten thousand words in a tongue. I thank my God I speak with tongues more than you all; Brethren, do not be children in understanding; however, in malice be babes, but in understanding be mature. Therefore if the whole church comes together in one place, and all speak with tongues, and there come in those who are uninformed or unbelievers, will they not say that you are out of your mind? But if all prophesy, and an unbeliever or an uninformed person comes in, he is convinced by all, he is convicted by all. And thus the secrets of his heart are revealed; and so, falling down on his face, he will worship God and report that God is truly among you. If anyone thinks himself to be a prophet or spiritual, let him acknowledge that the things which I write to you are the commandments of the Lord." I Corinthians 14:11-14,18-20,23-25,37

If we are mature, our hearts live for the lost and the unlearned, not to get our tongues speaking in a service. I truly believe people who try to punish their pastors for not letting them speak in tongues have hardly any personal walk with the Lord and are using the corporate anointing to lift themselves off the floor of life. That's not a statement of condemnation but just reality. Paul was the most mature and the most spiritual and he directed us to not all speak with tongues. I'm not embarrassed to be Spirit filled whatsoever, I'm just more in love with the souls of people who need to be saved and discipled then those who are saved and are just using Sundays to stay alive. What's the answer? Pray in tongues like Paul did, more than everyone else, just not in corporate meetings unless it's to bring an interpretation or you sense God is going to change it into another language to be a sign for an unbeliever. The heart is everything and my heart breaks to see people who are more devoted to their own experience than the ones who need it most. Like I said, if we are truly mature, we are speaking in tongues all week so in main services we will hear gifts of the Spirit in a known language in order that the church and unbelievers can be encouraged and saved. I truly believe it's a heart issue. It was always about the power of the Holy Spirit more than just focusing, even in services, on tongues.

On the other hand, I do believe that pastors should have discipled their people properly to allow the flow of the Holy Spirit and His gifts in the service. You can usually tell who is in the flesh, and we just approach those people personally to stop flesh movements. To be completely honest, those people who are in the flesh are alway angry at you for stopping their show. The Bible is explicit in what the Spirit of God is shown like: "Who is wise and understanding among you? Let him show by good conduct that his works are done in the meekness of wisdom. For where envy and self-seeking exist, confusion and every evil thing are there. But the wisdom that is from above is first pure, then peaceable, gentle, willing to yield, full of mercy and good fruits, without partiality and without hypocrisy. Now the fruit of righteousness is sown in peace by those who make peace." James 3:13,16-18 NKJV.

Honestly, we just approach people to let them know that we don't support practices or volumes that distract everyone else. As a pastor, I believe it's my responsibility to stop flesh and to allow the Spirit, even in the communicating of gifts of the Spirit. We can just be human. I love how Tomi Arayomi says it, *"[We are] teaching prophets to be people, and people to be prophets."* While we are not supposed to quench the Holy Spirit, we are not supposed to just let anything happen. That's not God either. But, instead of discipling the move of Jesus, for the most part, pastors have just saved it to a once a month service or really never, other than on paper. I am not condemning either or, this is just the state of the body right now, and if we have true wisdom, we aren't demanding, but in understanding, in love, and in humility, bring the move of God back again, in power.

I promise you right now, if you were to say Holy Spirit, fill me with power and change me to be a witness with sincerity, He would begin to fill you. Our appropriation of faith is everything. If you don't believe that He heals, you aren't healed. Many want the blessing of great men of God, but don't want to believe what they believed. They want an outpouring, but don't want the same sacrifice or faith Parham or Seymour had. They want healing like John G. Lake, but still want to believe God makes people sick. They want to see revival like Charles Finney, but they don't want to pray hours a day. We are looking for shortcuts. I believe the body of Christ has settled for tongues, because we settled for something less after the doctrine of tongues replaced power.

IT WAS NEVER BASED ON OUR PERSONALITIES, BUT ALWAYS BASED ON HIS POWER.

Why do so many believers suffer fear, depression, lukewarmness, and even moral depravity? No power. Because of this, a victim mindset has come into the church. Many mindsets facade a victim mindset. I believe they look like this: "I can't do this." "I can't do that," "It's not my gifting," " It's not my personality," "That's legalism," "That's pressure." What? Yes. It was never based on our personalities, but always about His power. It was never our limitations that limited His power, but our faith in His power. Hebrews 11 is a chapter of many people who were strengthened to do the miraculous and see the miraculous by their faith. It was never based on their skill set or talents. I don't think Samson had the ability to do pushups from birth. It wasn't like the disciples had a resume of healing the sick before they did. Even Paul had almost no discipleship training, but He learned to make disciples, heal the sick, raise the dead, relate to Gentiles, receive wisdom for parents, kids, and spouses when he wasn't married, didn't have kids nor was he a Gentile (some scholars think he was married; I get that, but His wisdom was out of experience) but he successfully reached out and God used what Paul said and did as the Word for us. By His power!

I fully understand the different giftings in Romans 12, Ephesians 4, and 1 Corinthians 12 and 14 but His commission and His power even went to Stephen a deacon,[81] gave an open vision to Ananais[82] about Paul, and used both men and women for the Gospel.[83] Jesus was God speaking to us. To say He was only talking to His disciples about the commission and the power is completely outlandish. This has been allowed in the church for God's people. We lower the level and then the power of God lowers. This book will bring some conviction but is really meant to give permission and answers to those who are wanting to see God's power. This is the answer to the church's fear; it's power. It will defeat fear and impart power, love, and boldness to every believer. We just need to surrender to His Way.

A SENDING ANOINTING

God's power came to make us burning bushes. What? Yes! Look at Exodus 3. Moses was attracted to a miracle; it was a burning bush that wasn't burning up. Our lives were to attract the lost into the presence of Jesus so they can be saved, and then sent. Encounters are waiting all day long. Many people are talking about God appointments, but they are missing them all day long. Our peers at work, the teller at Walmart, our friends, our neighbors, and even our family need to see miracles to completely believe the message. Even Moses almost didn't answer the call upon arriving at the burning bush and hearing from God. How much more do we need to be burning bushes of His power for the world to see and the church to be encouraged!

---

81 Acts 7
82 Acts 9
83 Romans 16

THE POWER CAME TO SEND US, NOT TO SIT US.

What an encounter, right? So many believers would love an encounter like this. It was almost face-to-face "as a man spoke to his friend," but then—the fire—the encounter spoke. It speaks to us today the same. That fire revealed to Moses how painful of a state his people were in. They were in oppression. That's what His power does. It makes us like Christ, with the heart of Christ, not just a doctrine. Many are gathering to encounter Jesus and hungry for His presence and I know God loves it; however, Biblically, God shows up so powerfully when it's for the purpose of being sent. This encounter with Moses and two of the biggest encounters in the New Testament were connected to people offering themselves to be sent. The power came to send us, not to sit us. I have had so many encounters since my first infilling, but it was along the way. I answered the call to be that burning bush for the church and the world. There are so many encounters in the Bible. Most of them accompanied people who were sent or for a purpose and not just looking for a feeling or encounter. I'm totally for this. I go to five or more conferences a year in addition to my personal time with Jesus to encounter Him, and I hunger greatly for more of Him; nevertheless, as soon as He came upon me, He sent me. His power gets our attention and then changes us to use us. All these people in the Bible didn't just have an esoteric gift, His power is for you!

The power of the Holy Spirit is available to all. As Jesus was to the disciples, He is to us. Jesus said, "You shall receive power when the Holy Spirit comes upon you, and you will be witnesses to Me in both Jerusalem, and in all Judea, and in Samaria, and to the uttermost parts of the earth," in Acts 1:8. I'll paraphrase,

"I'm sending power through the Holy Spirit so you can bring this Gospel with signs and wonders to the world." It was for a purpose, not a church gathering. I keep saying this, but people think I'm all stiff with evangelism but I'm just Biblical. Even in Acts 4, the disciples encountered persecution and asked God to send boldness, so they could preach the Gospel more. They asked Him to extend His hand with miracles, and then—BAM, God's power shook the house they were in and filled them again with power. God was so pleased with their request, He sent His power. God wants us to both feel His presence and be empowered that those who don't know Him may come to know Him through you.

This is the why of the church. If we don't understand why we meet, we lose the focus, the power, and everything. Most people think of the church as a place or an event on a day or two of the week, but it's a movement. This world isn't our reward. We can't camp out on trying to fill our lives with what everyone in this world does to be happy. This world will only last for a minute. Heaven is our reward. This is the why of the church. To seek and save the lost and to make fully devoted followers until we reach every person in this world. God's power is just the tool this is needed now more than ever. I pray you would allow the burning bush of God's heart to melt your heart to see that people are lost all around us and then take the first, second, third, and forever steps to see His kingdom come on earth.

You are the solution for heaven. Jesus sat down at the right hand of the majesty on high. He finished His work. It's now our job. He left love up to us. This world isn't our reward so we can give it up. This world isn't for us to enjoy, so we don't need to fit its mindset. Today, pray to God, ask Him to send His power upon you. Give your life to be a witness to His resurrection to the world around us. I only stay on fire when I'm reaching people for Him. Sure, preaching is okay, but seeing lives transformed by His power in sharing my faith or discipling those who are saved to do the same—now that's life. The Bible says, "The Spirit is willing, but the flesh is weak." Matthew 26:41. Today, if you can hear Him calling, pray this prayer, or something similar:

> *Father, I come to you in the name of Jesus Christ. I ask you to send your power upon me. I ask you to consume me with your power. I give up my mind, emotions, body, and life for your use. I'm sorry for using my life for myself and thinking your power was just for me. Here I am Lord, use me and spend me like a coin. I won't argue. I give the rest of my life for your power to send me and to spend me. Holy Spirit, come upon me with power. Quicken my life so I can glorify Jesus. Fill me with the same power the disciples had and all of those in church History. All for your glory. Amen.*

The greatest movement in history—Jesus and His church. It's all over the world! I believe that if you pray that, and keep praying that with all sincerity, He will answer in strength and power. I'm praying that he touches you and that His power and passion would fill every fiber of your being.

8.

I'M ANOINTED

I was on a live prayer and devotion hour for our ministry. I saw a vision in my spirit that someone had a dreadful fear of being alone in their home. A lady responded via the live feed. As soon as she replied she was the one with that fear, God showed me a broken-in door frame and He told me there was a break-in situation resulting in a near-death experience which left her afraid. I felt like taking the leap of faith to ask her while I was live on Facebook. She said two years prior, a guy broke in and tried raping her and ended up almost killing her. Since then, she has had that fear. She was touched as I began to pray. She said she felt God all over her ministering to her. Wow, God thinks about us and communicates through us! What a powerful God we serve! He has anointed #Every Believer to hear from Him and minister powerfully, even if it's on live video.

"The Spirit of the LORD is upon Me, Because He has anointed Me To preach the gospel to the poor; He has sent Me to heal the brokenhearted, To proclaim liberty to the captives And recovery of sight to the blind, To set at liberty those who are oppressed." Luke 4:18 NKJV

"Therefore, brethren, be even more diligent to make your call and election sure, for if you do these things you will never stumble." 2 Peter 1:10 NKJV

I've been around the world and what I've seen is the body of Christ who is anointed, yet they don't inherently believe they are anointed. I've met some of the most powerful prophetic or apostolic (believe in prophets, apostles, and miracles today) people who struggle with whether they are "called" or not. They are inside the most powerful of churches but after they walk out, it's like the Holy Spirit walked out too. They can pray for people in church, prophesy in a church, cast out demons in a church, sing in a church, or serve in a church, but outside the church they can't function. I truly believe it is just a lack of revelation to who the Holy Spirit is, what His role is, and why He is here. There is so much religion still in the church and we don't even know it. For some reason, people still are looking for permission to be powerful, and don't know that the same Holy Spirit that gave them tongues gave them power to hear from God, heal the sick, and send them to be a light into this world. He came to make us glow!

Not only did the Holy Spirit come to make church services powerful, He came to make the church powerful outside of the church services. Eighty-seven percent of all miracles done in the New Testament were done outside the church. The anointing that works inside the church works outside the church. The power that gives you the ability to preach in the church, gives the power to preach outside the church. The love the Holy Spirit gives to those in the church is in us to give outside the church. The confidence to pray for one another in the church is from the Holy Spirit and He's still alive outside the church. We have just been conditioned for "ministry" to be in the church, when the Holy Spirit literally came upon us to go outside the church. If we are anointed, it's for inside and outside the church. If people say they are only anointed for inside, I doubt that they are anointed at all! The Holy Spirit came for power to go, not just to sit!

The Bible says, *"if we make our calling and election sure,"*[84] we won't stumble. That means, we won't stumble in the church or out of the church. Is stumbling just sin or maybe being frozen in fear or not following through? It is super important to know what our calling is. What are we anointed to do? What does that mean? What can I expect God to do on my behalf? Who am I called to reach? These questions and more have plagued the church to the point it is paralyzed but they don't have to be anymore. I believe that the veil of confusion is coming off, and the church is rising to its finest hour.

Jesus said, *"the Spirit of the Lord is upon Me, BECAUSE..."*[85] (emphasis mine). What? The Holy Spirit came upon Jesus to EMPOWER Him to do what the Father sent Him to do. He didn't come onto Jesus just because He was hungry for more of God or because He wanted an experience with God. These are all good, but He came upon Jesus to carry out His mission. The primary reason for the Holy Spirit coming upon us isn't the reason most of us pursue Him, understand Him, or have experienced Him. The Holy Spirit came to send us, not to sit us. He came to make us anointed just like Christ, for a mission. I truly believe the most powerful days are ahead of the church because of this. When we come into alignment with the Holy Spirit's purpose and why He came, we come into position for His power to come upon us greater than we have ever seen and through us like we have never known.

---

84 2 Peter 1:10 NKJV
85 Luke 4:18; Isaiah 61:1 NKJV

Every car has its own purpose. A gas saver is to save gas. A sports car is to go fast. A family car is to tote family around. An off road vehicle is to go off road. A truck is to function primarily for towing, carrying, off-roading or for work-related uses. With all of these, the uses can be interchangeable, of course, but you will get the best bang for your buck within the original design for that vehicle. In the same way, the Holy Spirit comes upon us for a purpose, and until we come into agreement with that purpose, He will still be there, but just not as intended.

FOR THE MOST PART, THE BODY OF CHRIST THINKS BEING CHRIST-LIKE IS MEANT TO BE "NICE-LIKE" INSTEAD OF "ANOINTED-LIKE."

The Holy Spirit's greatest intent coming upon us was to anoint us like Christ. Even the word "Christian" means to be like Christ. That means, anointed like Christ. So many think being like Christ is to be nice like Christ, but Christ-like means to be anointed-like; Christ means anointed one. Christ-like would mean anointed like Christ. Jesus said, *"As the Father has sent me so I send you."*[86] He said, *"These works you shall do and even greater."*[87] He also said in what is known to be the first Gospel written, *"These signs will follow those who believe."*[88] Christ always intended for the commission with power to continue.[89] The church has thought that walking or looking like Christ meant to be "nice," like He was. For the most part, every reference I heard to being Christ-like when I was growing up meant being nice. As much as that is true, we are called to be powerful and anointed just like Christ.

86 John 20:21 NKJV
87 John 14:12 NKJV
88 Mark 16:15-18 NKJV
89 Matthew 28:18-20 NKJV

The future prophecy of the Messiah[90] revealed He would move in power. #Every Believer was promised the ability to move just like Him.[91] It is heaven's idea to anoint #Every Believer with His power, love, and a sound mind to draw everyone around us and encourage believers by His supernatural happenings. This can sound intimidating, but it starts by taking small steps. It takes big beliefs and times with God to confess and really get this into our spirits, but it only takes small steps of obedience. It's in your DNA and it's your promised land to move into this lifestyle.

THAT VICTIM MINDSET

The problem is the church has programmed everyone to think that our personal callings have nothing to do with Christ's commands. We have been conditioned to look for callings that suit our personalities rather than the calling of #Every Believer that is through His power. Most personalities and now, callings, are derived from pain, pain, and more pain and how to avoid pain in our lives. Then here comes Jesus who calls us all to share the Gospel and do what He did, and we get triggered because of that pain. But the promise of the Father was sent to empower us past our pain. The promise of the Father was to anoint us just like Jesus. It's based on His power and not on our pain nor our personalities. I do agree there are individual callings but callings from heaven don't cancel out the commission or the power that is given to every believer.

The church is a powder keg of God's power waiting to go off. The world hasn't seen it since the early church. The whole intent was for the Holy Spirit to make #Every Believer powerful.

---

90   Isaiah 11:1-5; Isaiah 61:1-3 NKJV
91   Mark 16:15-18 NKJV

The Old Testament was great but only a few were anointed to be leaders. In the last days, or in the New Covenant, He would pour out His power on all flesh. His power coming to the church was to make everyone powerful. It was to make everyone of us full of His love, hear His voice, and move in power.

The Holy Spirit baptizing you was God coming into you to stay. The Bible says Christ is called, "Emmanuel, God with us."[92] The Holy Spirit is to us as Christ was to the disciples. That means God's with you like Christ was with the disciples. He is with you as much as Christ was with the disciples and now, He's in you. The early disciples followed Christ and saw Him in the flesh, but really weren't changed until the Holy Spirit came into them. He turned them into different men. God was with them in the flesh, but now God was in them permanently. A bigger transaction has happened once you are born again and baptized in the Spirit, because now you have God with you. I mentioned this before, but Christ said, "As *the Father sent Me, so I send you*."[93] All that God asked Christ to do He backed up with His power and we are not sent empty handed. God Himself has anointed us. This means that He's with us everywhere we go, with power. Not just symbolically but with power. He is ready to back up this Gospel, His Way, His Son, with power.

OWNING THE ANOINTING

When we begin to own the anointing He has given us, we will be able to function in His power. The title of this chapter is called, "I'm Anointed." Why? Because most people are too timid to ad-mit to themselves they are anointed—never mind admitting that

92   Matthew 1:23 NKJV
93   John 20:21 NKJV

to others. Jesus was in the synagogue when He announced that He was anointed to heal, deliver, preach, etc. He was among haters too. Paul was able to say he was an apostle called by God. I believe we will begin to see the power of the Holy Spirit really cling to us when we own that we are anointed. You are powerful! If you have been baptized in the Holy Spirit and speak in tongues, power has come upon you; you are anointed. He came upon you for a reason, and for a purpose. He came to give you boldness, power, and love to represent Him everywhere. Part of being anointed is being confident in it. I have people say it out loud, "I am anointed." Try it. Sounds scary, right? But do it! Begin to change your belief system and your confession. I know, we have made the best speakers, singers, and guys who sit on stages to sound anointed, but you carry the same anointing as Jesus. You carry the same Holy Spirit. He didn't give you a lesser version of the Holy Spirit and then say you could do the same works. What if you began to say, "I'm anointed," or "I'm anointed to do what Christ did." David said this in Psalms 18:29 *NKJV: "For by You I can run against a troop, By my God I can leap over a wall."* It's in the Word, but he spoke it to Himself first before we were able to read it. There is something about speaking to ourselves and owning our anointing. I get it—you aren't anointed to go to the cross, because He was the only One who could have, but you are anointed to walk like He walked. If you begin to see this then you need to begin to say it. You are anointed!

There were two kings who had the same callings or anointing but only one of them succeeded. Both had the chance to be insecure. Saul was from the smallest tribe of Benjamin and his family was perhaps one of the least known.[94] At a minimum,

94 1 Samuel 9:21 NKJV

David wasn't one of the chosen of his father. David was possibly the son of a prostitute. What normally is used as a Scripture to represent we are all born in sin could have meant David was conceived in sin. (David's brothers were seemingly aristocrats, and we know Jesse's family was significantly well-off given their origins from Boaz's family as well as from the way they provided provisions for sons who were engaged in war at Saul's court). Either way, they both had reason to cling to insecurity. What was the difference? David took the calling of God personally. He let the prophecy truly run down into his heart to heal even his father's rejection or at the very last, his father's favoritism to his other brothers. I believe he killed the lion and the bear because he took it to heart.

Because of our wrong understanding of the baptism of the Holy Spirit, loose understanding of the idea of being anointed, and many of the false prophets around, I believe we are acting like Saul. I believe we aren't putting any weight in the fact that God's Holy Spirit has come to set us apart for service, for war. His Spirit was sent to anoint us to win battles just like David, but this time like Christ. The Holy Spirit is God's personal signet ring upon us. He has now granted us authority and power to do what He did. He gave us His name to be His ambassador in all of the world. If we don't take the callings and election of God personally instead of commercially, I believe we will be like Saul and so many others; we give up the God walk because of the fear of how people will talk. In the end, Saul knew his rule was over but still asked the prophet to sacrifice with him so the people could honor him. He was more concerned with how people saw Him than the calling of God being lifted off of him. The calling of God is precious. His Holy Spirit coming was only because His Son's blood was shed, so we need to accept our identity as anointed. Our hearts need to be won over by His power.

OUR SELF TALK IS SO IMPORTANT

The lady with the issue of blood demonstrates a principle that helped me and will help you breakthrough into your calling and move into the liberty of the Holy Spirit's promptings. There was a lady in Matthew 9 who had an irregular bleeding condition. She had sought for twelve years for the physicians' help but to no avail. *"For she said to herself, "If only I may touch His garment, I shall be made well." Matthew 9:21 NKJV.* The Bible says, "She said to herself." It didn't say God told her, simply that she spoke to herself. There were thousands, if not millions of miracles, but not too many individual accounts that were mentioned by Scripture, so it causes us to stop and take lessons from this woman. Let's just think about the sequence of events that may have happened.

At minimum, she heard about Christ. I'm sure she heard the good and the bad. She heard what was actually happening and what the religious were saying was happening. It was her choice to believe in the possibilities that made the difference. We hear about Christ and the power of Jesus too, but what happens next is important. She had the option to let her pain from the past dismiss this possibility of the present due to the rejection that could have taken place. This is our dilemma. The breakdown doesn't happen so much with our actual ability to believe. Instead, the problem lies in our *willingness* to believe. Some can say, "Well, she was desperate, there were no other options." That could be true, but I've met a lot of people who are hard-hearted and are in desperate situations. They have turned to doubt or even unbelief that nothing can heal them or deliver them—no matter what. Her story proves there is a need to release doubt and experience a new way.

Her heart began to open to the possibility of her situation looking like all the others she had heard. I'm sure she heard of deaf people hearing, blind people seeing, compassion for sinners, and more; instead of saying, "Nothing ever happens for me," or "That's only for some people," she took it personally. Whenever your heart begins to believe, your imagination and mouth begin to speak. I'm sure she saw herself touching His garment, but this wasn't enough. Dreaming is crucial to your experiencing breakthrough. Seeing yourself heal people, hearing from God, moving in compassion is so powerful, but what she did next, I believe, brought her to the tipping point. She spoke to herself, "If I just touch the hem of His garment, I'll be healed." Look, our heart believes, but sometimes—maybe more often than not, we need some encouragement. She didn't wait for others. She may have missed her blessing, if she waited for friends to encourage her. More than likely, her friends discouraged her or at the very least didn't encourage her. Many believers think that their pastors', friends', or close loved ones' support is conducive to their actions being ordained by God, but if we read the Word, that's not always true.

THE WAY WE TALK TO OURSELVES DETERMINES THE WAY WE MOVE OURSELVES.

Talking to yourself gives you strength to do what you haven't done before. This lady talked herself into a place that gave her strength to move forward. *However we talk to ourselves determines how we move ourselves.* I promise, when the Lord spoke to me to go and heal the sick again (it meant power evangelism or purposed power encounters); it's not like encouragement was the first thing to hit my emotions. To be honest, I live in a Baptist area. Our ministry as Spirit-filled believers was hard enough. When I had this revelation, I was pretty much alone in walking this out. I literally had to incorporate what this lady did. Our church looked at me like I was either out of my mind or just a cute little pastor doing this. My wife wasn't interested in this due to her past of rejection with being Spirit-filled. It was me and the Holy Spirit. Self-talk gave me the last bit of nudging that was needed to take steps of faith toward walking like Christ did, and it worked! It told myself over and over that I'm anointed; I told myself that the people I was going to be praying for were going to be healed, and that I could hear from God. I was talking to myself even as I was going into Walmart and surrounding stores. People asked me, "How did you not question yourself out of obeying?" I just said, "I talked myself through my fears." When your mouth is moving, your head is listening. I did this until my head stopped telling me the opposite.

Self-talk is important, and it was Biblical before it was in psychology. I'm sure when David was encouraging himself,[95] it wasn't just singing. I'm sure he was reminding himself he was anointed. Many times we remind ourselves or talk ourselves out of possibility, and you have to know it's the enemy at work. It was the enemy through our pain. I pray today, you would speak some Biblical and powerful confessions over yourself. The last thing the enemy wants is power encounters in the world.

---

95 1 Samuel 30:6 NKJV

I believe that, until there isn't hesitation, you will need to practice this. It seems contrary to customary practice, but it's mostly due to training that is geared to make you feel religious, not powerful. We've been trained by folks who don't take risks, who play it safe—and really, who don't look like the life of Jesus. As you begin to confess what God has already poured out on you, watch how boldness, security, and His power begins to fill you. I believe today, God could refresh and win your heart with His anointing if only you would come to Him again with an expectant heart. I'm praying for an outpouring of His power upon you and a revelation that His calling has single-handedly picked you!

FOUR TESTS OF BEING ANOINTED

And the Philistine drew near and presented himself forty days, morning and evening. So David rose early in the morning, left the sheep with a keeper, and took the things and went as Jesse had commanded him. And he came to the camp as the army was going out to the fight and shouting for the battle. And all the men of Israel, when they saw the man, fled from him and were dreadfully afraid. Then David spoke to the men who stood by him, saying, "What shall be done for the man who kills this Philistine and takes away the reproach from Israel? For who is this uncircumcised Philistine, that he should defy the armies of the living God?" And the people answered him in this manner, saying, "So shall it be done for the man who kills him." Now Eliab his oldest brother heard when he spoke to the men; Eliab's anger was aroused against David, and he said, "Why did you come down here? And with whom have you left those few sheep in the wilderness? I know your pride and the insolence of your heart, for you have come down to see the battle." And

David said, "What have I done now? Is there not a cause?" Then he turned from him toward another and said the same thing, and these people answered him as the first ones did. Then David said to Saul, "Let no man's heart fail because of him; your servant will go and fight with this Philistine." And Saul said to David, "You are not able to go against this Philistine to fight with him; for you are a youth, and he a man of war from his youth." But David said to Saul, "Your servant used to keep his father's sheep, and when a lion or a bear came and took a lamb out of the flock, I went out after it and struck it, and delivered the lamb from its mouth; and when it arose against me, I caught it by its beard, and struck and killed it. Your servant has killed both lion and bear; and this uncircumcised Philistine will be like one of them, seeing he has defied the armies of the living God." Moreover David said, "The Lord, who delivered me from the paw of the lion and from the paw of the bear, He will deliver me from the hand of this Philistine." And Saul said to David, "Go, and the Lord be with you!" So Saul clothed David with his armor, and he put a bronze helmet on his head; he also clothed him with a coat of mail. David fastened his sword to his armor and tried to walk, for he had not tested them. And David said to Saul, "I cannot walk with these, for I have not tested them." So David took them off. So the Philistine said to David, "Am I a dog, that you come to me with sticks?" And the Philistine cursed David by his gods. And the Philistine said to David, "Come to me, and I will give your flesh to the birds of the air and the beasts of the field!" Then David said to the Philistine, "You come to me with a sword, with a spear, and with a javelin. But I come to you in the name of the Lord of hosts, the God of the armies of Israel, whom you have defied. This day the Lord will deliver you into my hand,

and I will strike you and take your head from you. And this day I will give the carcasses of the camp of the Philistines to the birds of the air and the wild beasts of the earth, that all the earth may know that there is a God in Israel."

I Samuel 17:16, 20, 24, 26-30, 32-39, 43-46 NKJV

The first test is being anointed when nobody's looking. This principle is in Proverbs 25:28. It's something for a man or woman to truly accept the call and the anointing of God. It takes us going home after we have received the Spirit to know that we know He is with us. You know David was with those sheep but he was meditating on Samuels words. I'm sure he was wrestling every insecurity down with that promise. "I'm called, I'm anointed, God's With Me, I can take anything down," kind of statements. Then David tackles a bear and a lion when nobody's looking. Unbeknownst to him, this will provide a backbone to his faith when he has to stand in front of everyone. When you receive the anointing, He gets you started by prompting you to pray for someone, to share the Gospel, or to do something. It's these many attempts to obey God, when nobody is looking, that prepares you to lead others into battle when God puts you into that position. If you are regularly doing this, and staying pure, you can best believe leadership will be soon.

The second is in front of family and friends. David's brother accused him of evil despite personally seeing David anointed by the prophet. I know they should support you, but this foreknowledge will save you from hurt. The devil uses those closest to you to stop the Jesus in you. Family and friends are often one of the hardest critics when we do these things. By this time, we should have owned our Christ-like anointing so much so, that if your family challenges it, it won't throw you off. This principle is mentioned in 1 Timothy 3:5. Our family is usually the hardest because we respect them the most, and they really should be supporting the life of Christ more than anyone, but they mostly won't. That doesn't mean we have to be defensive and be rash with family; we just need to be confident that God is with us and start to let our private life come into our families lives.

WE ARE CALLED BY GOD, NOT INVITED BY MAN.

The third test is before leaders. Yes, leaders in the body. The king of Israel told David to his face that he wasn't equipped or legitimate to take down Goliath. But David was ready. His heart was so secure in the promise and anointing he received, he could tell the king his testimony instead of shutting down. Your anointing is enough. This is why it's important to really step out before you are invited. We are called by God, not invited by man. This doesn't mean we create division in our churches or come against leadership when they don't understand. My advice is that you don't take direction from any rejection you receive. They may not like that you heal the sick, prophesy, or cast out demons. They may not like the fact you reach the lost, but it's your calling, not your invitation. It's the mandate of heaven. I always say this, there are over seven billion people outside of your local ministry to talk or minister to. This is the true test of the heart. If you can go with nobody looking, if you can function in front of your family, if your leaders are not with you, and your heart stays pure and you still slay, you are on stomping grounds with the greats.

The last real test is the enemy. Goliath tried to intimidate David, but David was ready for him too. There may be a situation or two that, on the outside, looks intimidating, but remember your private time victories. Remember the lion, the bear, and then Goliath will fall. Give yourself ten times more grace than you think you need, and Goliath will fall. My first time leaving the country was a little intimidating. I did it by faith because I had seen about seven hundred folks healed by then. You would think it would be easier overseas, but it's not. It's all in our mind. Time in the presence of Jesus and truly going over miracles that happened here in the USA helped me get strength to go to a whole new nation. It will work. Just hang in there. The Holy Spirit was more for David than he knew and is more for you than you know.

You're anointed! If the Holy Spirit has come upon you, you are anointed. God is with you and backing you like He backed His Son. He's not backing us because we are asking or trying to be special, but this is His plan and has been His plan since Christ came. His plan was to make #Every Believer supernatural so the whole world could know Him. The Holy Spirit takes the power, boldness, and gifts that were on Jesus and imparts that grace to #Every Believer. Jesus paved the Way to a new era where it wouldn't be the one or two, but it would be #Every Believer anointed to walk like He did. I'm praying for you to see His dream, to be filled with His ability, and for His love to express Himself through you.

9.

PRACTICE MAKES ~~PERFECT~~ POWERFUL

After I had the encounter with Christ which gave me permission to just be powerful now, I started heading out anywhere I could ask people to allow me to pray for them for any pain they had. If I saw a vision, I would ask the recipient if it was relevant to them. Although this was a great start and people were healed, I felt as though I was supposed to create a goal to get over myself and my fears that had accumulated over the years. So I said to myself, "I won't go home until I see five people are healed." I had it in my mind to ask them several times and communicate that I wasn't here to make me feel special, but for them to be honest with their symptoms. I went out to stores all over my area and started to stop people and ask if I could pray, and sometimes I would have words of knowledge as well; I didn't go home until five people a day had been healed and had encountered God.

These actions were one of the biggest keys to breaking me through my mind and heart with power and boldness to share my faith and minister with words of knowledge. I believe that the biggest missing component of the Christian walk is training or practice. It literally makes you powerful. Why are the best armies in the world full of the hardest training? Does winning

Gold medals in the Olympics have more to do with their eight hours of training than it does with their talent? Are the majority of business men just lucky or hardworking and willing to take risks nobody else is? In the same way, are the people moving in the Spirit and seeing more of God move only through their gifts? Or—maybe they have practiced?

FINDING INDIVIDUALITY HAS REPLACED FOLLOWING CHRIST.

In other words, it's discipleship. Discipleship is one of the biggest foundations in the body of Christ, but yet we don't do it as much anymore so we don't cause offense. Everyone wants individuality so much that we don't follow Christ. Everybody wants the blessing of Abel with the sacrifice of Cain. They have no skin in the game. But training is before the promise and it's preparation for provision. Jesus said, "Go and make disciples." That means to put them into the same training He put them in. Most people will hear the Word and think it's just supposed to work, rather than practice it until it works. So many think that Jesus and the early disciples came for a one time show to wow the masses or to be worshiped, but they came as examples that would break the limitation off of our lives. Jesus was the Lamb of God—yes, but He still came as a human to die for all humans. He was empowered by the same Holy Spirit, and still told His disciples to teach them to observe everything He commanded them to do. It was a training exercise that would be foundational for the church to repeat itself, so it would be the greatest movement ever. It's still possible!

UNDIVIDED PERSUASION

I was in a high school outreach club when all of this started to break out. I had seen a few hundred healed by that time, and I was excited to see more healings. I asked for prayer requests and a girl asked for prayer for her grandma. She had stage four terminal cancer. So I said, "It will go." I prayed with all my heart and told her to let me know next week. The next week, she came in but the report was still the same. I said, "Don't worry, we will pray again." We prayed again, and I said, "Tell me what's happening next week." The third week was the same and I responded the same. The fourth week she came back and said her Grandma was cleared from cancer! She said the doctors couldn't explain it, that all of a sudden the cancer went into remission on its own. Wow! Miracles can happen if we don't give into doubt, ego, or just weariness. Early on, the Lord showed me that prayer and enforcing the supernatural was just like Israel versus the enemies in the Promised Land. We shouldn't give up or give in to the enemies in our land. So many people have been healed after the third or fourth prayer. I encourage you to press in beyond your fears, beyond your failings, beyond not seeing God show up, beyond your not hearing God—until you do. The reward is unspeakable.

The reward for your persistence is breakthrough and blessing! Here's the problem: religion has capped the wells of the miraculous just like the Philistines capped the wells of Abraham. As you read the passage below, I hope you see yourself as Isaac and religion as the Philistines and corrupt shepherds. This is the problem! We feel like we are doing something new, but we are uncovering that which was given and developed for us.

The hardship we are seeing and encountering is due to the corporate body accepting the lack of wells (miracles) as a normal thing. The culture of modern Christianity has made it really difficult for you and me to really push forward with the miraculous. I don't believe that unbelieving Christians are like the Pharisees, but are blinded by that spirit. The life #Every Believer is called and promised to live is being fought by our modern Christianity, and we have a hidden belief that the majority determines what's right, but there is a reward for those who are persistent. There is a reward for those who believe there is water where Abraham dug. There is breakthrough if you just persist. Diligence is a hard thing to put into practice, but God rewards those who diligently seek Him.[96]

"But without faith it is impossible to please Him, for he who comes to God must believe that He is, and that He is a rewarder of those who diligently seek Him." Hebrews 11:6 NKJV

Then Isaac sowed in that land, and reaped in the same year a hundredfold; and the Lord blessed him. The man began to prosper, and continued prospering until he became very prosperous; for he had possessions of flocks and possessions of herds and a great number of servants. So the Philistines envied him. Now the Philistines had stopped up all the wells which his father's servants had dug in the days of Abraham his father, and they had filled them with earth. And Abimelech said to Isaac, "Go away from us, for you are much mightier than we."

Then Isaac departed from there and pitched his tent in the Valley of Gerar, and dwelt there. And Isaac dug again the wells of water which they had dug in the days of Abraham his father,

---

96 Hebrews 11:6 NKJV

for the Philistines had stopped them up after the death of Abraham. He called them by the names which his father had called them.

Also Isaac's servants dug in the valley, and found a well of running water there. But the herdsmen of Gerar quarreled with Isaac's herdsmen, saying, "The water is ours." So he called the name of the well Esek, because they quarreled with him. Then they dug another well, and they quarreled over that one also. So he called its name Sitnah. And he moved from there and dug another well, and they did not quarrel over it. So he called its name Rehoboth, because he said, "For now the Lord has made room for us, and we shall be fruitful in the land." Genesis 26:12-22 NKJV

The problem with persistence is that everyone's time table and breakthrough points are at a different pace. I can't tell you when you will breakthrough, I can only tell you that you will breakthrough if you don't give up. Again, our pain of rejection, upbringing, circumstances, lack of moral support, etc. will all scream, trying to get you to give up. It's not time to give up, but find a friend who will cry with you, pray with you, and then get you back up again. This is what you were made for. I understand there will be definition in everyone's calling, but it never cancels out the calling and possibility for #Every Believer to prophesy, heal the sick, cast out demons, share the Good News, and make disciples. The problem is, our flesh would prefer us to give up and take a lesser calling or level of power for our lives. As you continue to follow Christ, practice, and tell yourself it's okay to fail, you will begin to see your faith become rock solid.

FOUNDED ON THE ROCK

Growing up in a Spirit-filled church, I frequently heard people saying to be founded on the Rock, or that they were founded on the Rock. "I'm founded on the Rock, Greg." I understand that could be quoted from Matthew 16:18, when Peter had the revelation that Jesus was the Christ, but I want to present a different option. I truly believe the church has been swindled out of power and its foundation by this terminology. Now, before you shut me out, I truly believe that Jesus is the Rock, the foundation of the church, not just a prayer to pray, but a life we could live. You've read up until now, so I believe you could see that. I want to challenge you that being founded on the Rock has more to do with application than just a good doctrine. There is so much INFORMATION available today it's really incredible. There are millions of sermons, thousands of preachers and teachers, but not many followers. This Scripture really changed my life in how I see that terminology:

"Therefore whoever hears these sayings of Mine, and does them, I will liken him to a wise man who built his house on the rock: and the rain descended, the floods came, and the winds blew and beat on that house; and it did not fall, for it was founded on the rock. But everyone who hears these sayings of Mine, and does not do them, will be like a foolish man who built his house on the sand: and the rain descended, the floods came, and the winds blew and beat on that house; and it fell. And great was its fall." Matthew 7:24-27 NKJV

I've stated before and even shown that doctrine is important to how we experience Christ but even more important than that, is the application of His Word. I believe we have a church that thinks learning something is the same as practicing that revelation in God's site. But clearly, here, Jesus says that the doers of His Word, not just Moses', but His, are what makes us founded on the Rock. I want to present a Way that would build you up so strong, that no matter the storm, you will not fail. This could almost be said, that what I'm about to tell you is a secret of faith. That faith isn't a panic button we push in times of emergency, but a muscle built through a relationship with the One who gives that faith.

This truly supports the phrase, "practice makes powerful." The more we act out our faith the more we will see testimonies. The more we see testimonies, the deeper our faith goes. The deeper our faith goes, the more we are ready for any storm that comes our way. This will get personal but it's so powerful. There are so many that like healing because it speaks of future protection for our family; however, without consistent application, the revelation of that healing will lose its strength for that future hope. I meet so many people who don't know this, and, honestly, I don't know if people will like this. Just like fasting brings health to our bones and people still don't apply it, so does this principle prepare us. The more we practice the deeper and stronger our faith gets. People are being misled to think that just because they hear a message, it eternally drives that faith inside of their hearts. Faith is like a muscle, it must be used. The more I use the gifts God gives, the more I see miracles, the more testimonies I hear, and because of it, the more I am ready for my own family's needs.

This really speaks of a greater issue. Most of us are using the goodness of God for us, our families, and our loved ones and not for His kingdom. It's really the opposite and that's why hardly anyone sees power, healing, or hears from God in times of trouble. Most people are about attending but not practicing. They are not about His kingdom. They are not doing what Jesus said to do. Do you realize that hearing from God on purpose for others prepares you to hear from God for later when you may need it? Healing the sick for His kingdom, not ours, gives us faith for when our families need it? That ministering to people with no strings attached prepares us to minister to our families? But we have it backwards and nobody sees it. We attend a sermon or service, hear of His amazing goodness, but nobody goes out afterwards to practice what they just heard preached. The Word was never meant to just be heard. Even in this parable, hearing the goodness of God didn't protect the foolish servant; it was when the wise man applied, practiced, and obeyed the words of Christ regularly that stabilized his own home. Can I go a little deeper now? Our families are suffering from unbelief and some kids are even leaving the faith, because they have never seen Jesus in the house or outside of the house. We are asking them to believe in a Jesus we don't even practice. How many homes show love, forgiveness, power practiced regularly to outsiders, or hearing from God regularly? Hardly any. So what have we been doing? We have been telling our kids to believe in a message that we aren't practicing. They hear a prayer to pray but do not see a life to live. They hear Jesus is the Way, but mom and dad are always contentious. They hear that they should love their neighbors, but their parents are gossiping or griping about ours. They hear about God's power in church, but hear us talking about how Jesus doesn't heal anymore.

If the church had been practicing Jesus, no storm in hell could kill our families. Okay, I know, now what? Well, we just need to make it right. God overlooks our times of ignorance but now commands us to repent.[97] It's our time. As a parent, I'm always apologizing when I miss it. I have to. My kids have to see a repentant heart. Although I'm not perfect, I'm still representing a heart like David. This Way, that is, the Jesus Way, changed my heart, changed my life, so I must follow Christ for His kingdom—not my comfort. It's what truly protects our families. They must see it and taste it personally.

This is even connected to HOW our faith develops. The Bible says, "faith works through love."[98] That love that's described here is "agape." There are four different Greek words to describe love in the Bible. *Eros* is used to described romantic or erotic love. *Philia* is a friendship focused love. *Storge* is used mostly to describe a love between family. Lastly, *agape* love. In Galatians 5:6, Paul uses *agape* love to describe that which faith works for. Even faith hinges on us moving in selfless love to grow our faith. That means to regularly use our faith towards people that will not benefit us. What? Yes. People who are just using the promises of God for themselves and their families are not reaching the fullest expression of faith; if it's not *agape*, it may not be producing that much faith at all. Hold on a second. Just think about it; the prosperity Gospel has been misinterpreted, making people think God's will for all of us is that we prosper, more than it is to follow Him. He has promised us things, but that was not to be OUR goal in life. If our hearts are with Him, we follow Him, and His promises are just trust factors, not consuming our daily thoughts. The one thing Jesus said not to do, we do—worry. If our hearts are engaged for His kingdom, then

97   Acts 17:30 NKJV
98   Galatians 5:6 NKJV

faith is a natural byproduct. What? Faith works through *agape* love. When we follow a love that doesn't even think of us, that is, for His kingdom, and His people, faith is easily cultured. I'm not even talking about families. That's *storge*, the Greek word for family love. This will get real, but I've met drug dealers, prostitutes, and many unsaved people that want their families provided for, healed, and taken care of. They even pray to a God that these things would happen. Why do I mention this? I believe that somewhere, obedience to the body of Christ has looked radical to believe by faith for our needs, our families' needs, and those around us. That is a great witness but wasn't the end goal. He said to seek first His kingdom, that is, the lost and those needing discipling more than ours. Our kingdom entails the things and people we count as special to us. It's special to God but its speciality was never supposed to eclipse our commission to reach the world with His power and love.

I have a healing training that activates every believer to be able to heal the sick, and the application that follows to see the best results. The pattern I see though is that people try to take the training for THEIR loved ones and not for Christ's kingdom. They don't take it to reach and disciple those that don't profit them, just those that would benefit THEIR purpose. It's not wrong, but this wasn't supposed to be our focus. I always tell people, you don't want to take this for your family first, but for His Kingdom. Why? Faith works through *AGAPE*, or that love that gives that doesn't benefit me. The "Founded on the Rock" principle really makes a difference. It eventually benefits home, but there are no shortcuts; it's for His kingdom. It's the New Testament. The New Testament was the pattern to follow. The church (#Every Believer) was to be the light of the world. I've heard people say, "If God heals my family members, then I'll pray for others," as if God has to do that to win me in order for me to heal or disciple others. The problem is that we weren't doing His commission even before our family members were sick. It's backwards. We follow His commission or His training first, then it benefits home.

Faith isn't a panic button we push in times of emergency but a muscle that is developed by a relationship of revelation and obedience with the Father. Imagine if you knew you were going to have to run a marathon or lift a really big weight to save your family. I mean, at any time in the next few years this may happen. You would begin to exercise to be ready right? You would prepare. The Bible says, "Be diligent to present yourself approved to God, a worker who does not need to be ashamed, rightly dividing the word of truth." 2 Timothy 2:15 NKJV. I believe that one of the biggest blunders in the body of Christ is the notion that hearing His Word a few times about a subject equips us for that fight. It doesn't. It's like studying about the marathon or lifting of weights but not preparing. This Scripture shows it all. It speaks of diligence. If we aren't diligent enough to prepare then we will be ashamed. It would be like showing up at that marathon or weight lifting competition saying you studied this or prayed about it when we had the time and life to train to prepare. It says we need to study and train so we aren't ashamed. I truly believe that, if we were to purposely train, we would begin to see a reversal of much of what happens in so many lives, because our faith would be ready for what life throws at us.

I'm not saying God doesn't show up sovereignly, but wouldn't it be awesome if we had thousands of obedience testimonies rather than the odd sovereign testimony? Being a son of God looks like Jesus. Flexing our muscles outside the church and family or friends is the kingdom; it is the foundation that provides stability to our personal storms. When we train, yes theologically, but practically, we will see the strength of God surge through us. Yes, I've had sovereign acts of God as well, but most of the testimonies I see are just plain obedience to what the Father already asked and displayed through Christ. Training outside of what benefits us is what strengthens and develops our faith to be ready for any storm that comes our way. Isn't praying for the sick, casting demons out, opening blind eyes, rescuing those who are lost, and discipling believers just stopping storms for everyone else in this world? It's the act of Agape love to this world. It doesn't benefit us today but prepares us for tomorrow.

1 Corinthians 9:25 "Everyone who competes in the games exercises self-control in all things. They then do it to receive a perishable crown, but we an imperishable."

Training makes you like a machine; it sets us apart. I always say, "Practice makes you powerful; it doesn't make you perfect." Practicing the power of the Holy Spirit, hearing from God, going up to complete strangers is what set my soul free. It was the training that Jesus made His disciples do. When we push our feelings out of the way by purposeful practice, it covers all of the triggers we have dealt with. I like to practice until there is no argument in my flesh anymore. It makes you a machine. Why do NFL teams still practice the basics? Why does the military hold basic training? Why do the trades have apprenticeships and not just learning? It's to cause our bodies and minds to have a consistent response to things that will still cause us to live and to win in life. This is what training does. It beats our bodies and emotions into submission so that when the Spirit speaks, there is no argument. It truly makes us a power, love, and sound mind machine; it makes you powerful.

PRACTICE MAKES YOU POWERFUL; IT DOESN'T MAKE YOU PERFECT.

"But I discipline my body and make it my slave, so that, after I have preached to others, I myself will not be disqualified." 1 Corinthians 9:27 NKJV

Grace is free but your training isn't. Many say grace is free and that thought seems theologically correct, but it still costs someone something, just not the trainee at the moment. But when it's our training, or—let me say, our completion—it costs. I say completion, because training, until we breakthrough, is what completes us as men or women of God.

I understand this is not complementary to our flesh, but when was that ever a reason to not develop ourselves? Victim mind-sets have invaded the body of Christ, where everyone is a victim of their situations rather than a follower of their God. Self-control is a fruit of the Holy Spirit. It is self-discipline. We live in the age of convenience, and it has ruined much of the body of Christ. People live by the mentalities of "If it's for me it would just happen," or, "I tried that once." Jesus' living and Jesus' faith were not on trial—it's a conviction. Faith is the CONVICTION that something we believe is true.[99]

Have you ever met someone convicted of anything? You can't persuade them. It's a core value in their life. I was in the

---

99 Hebrews 11:1 ESV

Philippines with Pastor Richard Conte, one of my favorite people. We were having a coffee, and I noticed a Middle Eastern man sitting outside of the coffee shop on the chairs and tables provided. I said, "I'm going to go talk to that man." I went over to strike up a conversation with him about Jesus and introduced myself. He was a Jew from Israel. He was in the Philippines on a business trip. There was nothing wrong with his body, so I just shared the testimony of how Yeshua had changed my heart and life and what we were seeing around the world to confirm His message. I said, "What are you thinking hearing me?" He said, "I believe you." I said, "What?" I was totally surprised. He said, "I don't meet too many people who believe to their core what they are saying." He said, "I can see you are totally persuaded in what you are talking about." He didn't come to Christ right there, but said he would seriously take this conversation to heart. It was really a great conversation. The point I'm making is conviction. If we have a conviction, it drives us to follow it. If we are persuaded about Christ, it doesn't matter if it's our flesh, Roman soldiers threatening our lives, the cancel culture society that wants to make us look like monsters, or worse, we will follow Him thoroughly.

"We do not want you to become lazy, but to imitate those who through faith and patience inherit what has been promised" Hebrews 6:12 NKJV

OVERCOMING FEAR

My first healing ever was the time I was walking around with my friends in Lethbridge, Alberta, Canada, talking about Paul and Silas and how they preached the Gospel with boldness. Up until then, I would share my faith—if I mustered up the confidence—with a few people, but I hadn't openly preached the Gospel. As we were talking about the New Testament disciples, my friend challenged me and said, "Why don't you do it then?" Fair enough, here I was leading a prayer walking session and talking about power, so I guess I should have been. Now the pressure was on. (Technically, there is no pressure, but at that point, I still had that little boy part that had to follow up on that challenge). My heart was pounding and fear seemed to appear out of nowhere. But I just took the step and then—bam—God showed up. As soon as I opened my mouth to preach all I knew about the Gospel of Jesus, I sensed boldness surge through my emotions. I just kept preaching; it was a breakthrough. Then a man who was walking bent over came over to ask what I was doing, and I told him. I saw him walking in pain, so I asked what was wrong. He said his back was hurting. So we prayed. Power! He straightened up and said his pain went away. Wow! It was my first healing, my first real step of boldness. I believe the same will happen with you!

Wow, one of the biggest challenges to overcoming fear is being baptized in the Holy Spirit. After that, the mindset the Lord gave me really got me over taking the leap and got me to start taking consistent steps of faith. This Scripture and revelation will free you from the fear that seems to paralyze so many:

"Then Elisha said, "Listen to the word of the LORD; thus says the LORD, 'Tomorrow about this time a measure of fine flour will be sold for a shekel, and two measures of barley for a shekel, in the gate of Samaria.'" The royal officer on whose hand the king was leaning answered the man of God and said, "Behold, if the LORD should make windows in heaven, could this thing

be?" Then he said, "Behold, you will see it with your own eyes, but you will not eat of it." Now there were four leprous men at the entrance of the gate; and they said to one another, "Why do we sit here until we die? If we say, We will enter the city, then the famine is in the city and we will die there; and if we sit here, we die also. Now therefore come, and let us go over to the camp of the Arameans. If they spare us, we will live; and if they kill us, we will but die." They arose at twilight to go to the camp of the Arameans; when they came to the outskirts of the camp of the Arameans, behold, there was no one there. For the Lord had caused the army of the Arameans to hear a sound of chariots and a sound of horses, even the sound of a great army, so that they said to one another, "Behold, the king of Israel has hired against us the kings of the Hittites and the kings of the Egyptians, to come upon us." Therefore they arose and fled in the twilight, and left their tents and their horses and their donkeys, even the camp just as it was, and fled for their life. When these lepers came to the outskirts of the camp, they entered one tent and ate and drank, and carried from there silver and gold and clothes, and went and hid them; and they returned and entered another tent and carried from there also, and went and hid them. Then they said to one another, "We are not doing right. This day is a day of good news, but we are keeping silent; if we wait until morning light, punishment will overtake us. Now therefore come, let us go and tell the king's household." So they came and called to the gatekeepers of the city, and they told them, saying, "We came to the camp of the Arameans, and behold, there was no one there, nor the voice of man, only the horses tied and the donkeys tied, and the tents just as they were." The gatekeepers called and told it within the king's household.

Then the king arose in the night and said to his servants, "I will now tell you what the Arameans have done to us. They know that we are hungry; therefore they have gone from the camp to hide themselves in the field, saying, 'When they come out of the city, we will capture them alive and get into the city.'" One of his servants said, "Please, let some men take five of the horses which remain, which are left in the city. Behold, they will be in any case like all the multitude of Israel who are left in it; behold, they will be in any case like all the multitude of Israel who have already perished, so let us send and see." They took therefore two chariots with horses, and the king sent after the army of the Arameans, saying, "Go and see." They went after them to the Jordan, and behold, all the way was full of clothes and equipment which the Arameans had thrown away in their haste. Then the messengers returned and told the king. So the people went out and plundered the camp of the Arameans. Then a [measure of fine flour was sold for a shekel and two measures of barley for a shekel, according to the word of the LORD. Now the king appointed the royal officer on whose hand he leaned to have charge of the gate; but the people trampled on him at the gate, and he died just as the man of God had said, who spoke when the king came down to him. It happened just as the man of God had spoken to the king, saying, "Two measures of barley for a shekel and a measure of fine flour for a shekel, will be sold tomorrow about this time at the gate of Samaria." 2 Kings 7:1-20 NKJV

I call this, "the mindset of lepers." There was a famine in the land, but if you know God, there is always a "find", in the famine! We just have to be the ones with the right mindset. This mindset can bring us to where solutions exist. In this current state of the church it looks like a famine but there is a find. Just like the rest of Israel in this situation, most of the church is frozen in fear of what is around us rather than WHO is for us. In this passage there was a miracle waiting for ANYONE who would cross their fear. Just the same, there is a miracle waiting for you, if you cross the threshold everyone else in the body of Christ is afraid to cross! The Lord of the Harvest is WAITING to give to those who will live by RISK. Those who will be like the lepers.

They knew they were going to die anyway, so their mindset that helped them get over their fear was this: "We are going to die anyways." Wow—so simple, but so profound. Death, pain, rejection, etc. will come anyway. Regardless of whether we do right or wrong, pain comes. Ten out of ten people will die according to statistics. Ten out of ten people encounter rejection, betrayal, failure, etc. whether or not they do what's safe, wrong, or right, so why not live on the faith side of taking risks for Christ instead of being like everyone else, who were and are dying anyway? There is a famine of God's glory in the land, and He needs people who are different than the world and cultural levels of comfort in church society.

Look, death isn't pleasant. Rejection isn't pleasant. Fear isn't pleasant, but dying sitting here, or—even worse—dying afraid of the thing you always knew to do, is worse. The lepers were the least likely people to win the war, but they were the best choice according to God. Their past pain actually helped them come to this point. You can either use your past pain as motivation to move forward, or stay where you are, but only moving forward in faith wins the game of destiny.

You will die anyway. What? One of the things that fear does is threaten us with what could happen. Well, it's time to answer that fear. Fear not dealt with doesn't go away. This principle pretty much means, "What we fear could possibly happen anyway, so I might as well incur it doing things the right way, the Christ Way." People will reject us anyway, so we might as well receive that rejection living the Jesus Way. Just think of it, all those compromises to be cool, to be accepted by friends and family, and yet still rejection, still abandonment, still pain! No matter what, fear never works for anyone!

Fear is from the enemy; it's a lie, and it's not actually going to protect us. For some reason, the enemy has convinced us if we just pull the covers over our head it will save us from devastation. Truth is, if there is a boogie man, the covers won't help you. When I was a child I truly believed that if I just covered myself with covers and stayed deathly still, the boogie man wouldn't hurt me, and I was right, he didn't. Why, because he wasn't real and if he was, I wouldn't be here. I'd be gobbled up. But, in this world, pain is real, but our attempts to avoid it are not worthy of their attempts, attention, or time we give them. What? Fear has the idea that if I just stay away from things that trigger past pain, that pain won't happen again. I understand that there is wisdom in keeping away from foolish pain, but following Christ, training, and being discipled is good pain. Bad pain is just allowing things to happen accidentally in life. Good pain is when we take charge of our emotions and begin to think like the lepers. That is part of what counting the cost looks like. Though I walk through the valley of past pains and fears, I will fear no evil. We need to take His Word personally.

Clarity really helps. We need to see that faith and fear are very similar. They are both expecting something to happen that hasn't happened yet. One is negative or pain based and the other is love or God based. Faith believes God's side of the story, whereas fear believes the devil's side of your story. It threatens to repeat past pain over and over and over again. I encourage you to ask the Lord to pinpoint what fears are keeping you from following His voice that is trying to make you powerful. These fears keep us in an illusion that the pain is abnormal. It's really crazy, I truly believe we are the first generation that believes to the core this world was here for us. We actually believe comfort is normal. But historically, chaos and pain is a normal part of this world. We paint the goodness of God towards lives that are easier rather than the price He paid at the cross for our sins. Convenience has made a mindset where we truly believe that if it's God's will, it would be easier. Like, if I'm truly called to this or that, it would be more convenient. This is why I believe we are in a blur of danger, all the while believing something is wrong, because pain has been involved or there is chaos in our pictures. Are there promises? Yes. Are there benefits? Yes. Is there prosperity? Yes. But all those weren't supposed to be our goal or priority for life. Jesus being preached and His Way duplicated was the sole goal of the New Testament church but now, our comfort seems to be the goal. I truly believe that if we can allow the Holy Spirit to adjust our perspectives, His power will move more powerfully in our daily lives and places we lead for Christ.

This world was not meant to protect us. I understand, nobody warned us of pain in this world, and that's what makes it even worse. Nobody likes surprises but this world isn't supposed to treat us right. We were born in a war ship not in a cruise ship.

There is a real devil that uses real people. His intent was to wound you when you were young and unsuspecting, so that by the time Jesus comes knocking, we think we are being wise to say, "No way." I'm truly sorry for your pain, but it became the new normal after Adam sinned. With sin came pain, and, contrary to popular belief, our goal in life isn't to be safe, prosper, or comfortable; it is to be the light of the world no matter the fear that tries to hold us back.

THIS WORLD IS NOT MY REWARD

One of the biggest revelations that helps us get over ourselves is simply, "This world is not our reward." Most think that God owes them instead of realizing that He owns us. He didn't save us to give us a good life here, but to use us to win others to Him. If we can realize that nothing in this world is my reward or made for me, we can get over our distractions and disagreements with following Christ. My comfort, my convenience, my ease of life, my feelings being right, my wife, my children, etc. are not my reward. "Wait, the Word promises these things!" Yes, but they are not a priority for us nor a waiting place before we follow the Lord, they are just benefits while we sojourn through this planet, until we see Him face to face.

"Then He said to them all, 'If anyone desires to come after me, let him deny Himself, and take up his cross daily, and follow Me.'" Luke 9:23

"And they overcame him by the blood of the Lamb and by the word of their testimony, and they did not love their lives to the death." Revelation 12:11 NKJV

Did that say *death*? Whew—training isn't fun. Another hindrance to training is the faulty thinking that the will of God or obedience to God or what God would have me do has to feel good. People think that it's supposed to be complementary with our personality, but it's not; it's complementary with His will. That's what makes people unholy. "God would want me to be happy," "God would want me to do this," and more statements that empower our flesh instead of understanding that God would want me to train and be the best at this. It's totally worldly, but the devil has tricked the church to think it's holy. The biggest enemy to our future self is the comfort involved in who we are right now. Training is everything if reaching our goal is a priority. Set goals that consistently get you out of your comfort levels. It will seem like death is imminent, but it's the beginning of the real you resurrecting.

GRACE AND THE GOODNESS OF GOD DOESN'T REPLACE OUR OBEDIENCE, IT'S STRENGTHENS IT.

How do we overcome the devil? We have to do the opposite of what the modern church is doing. We have been given a convenient and needs-based Gospel. What? Yes, God's primarily our provider over Him being Lord or even Savior. We focus on the blood of the Lamb and the word of our testimony from Revelation 12:11, but why not loving our lives not to the death? We sing songs about this, train our people in the power of the blood, but not in the power of loving our lives not to death. I want to propose that the majority of the problem in the church has less to do with the devil than our self-serving mentalities. I am totally for and love the teaching of the blood of the Lamb and the power of testimony. It protects us, encourages us, blesses us, strengthens us, and heals us. The problem is it was never meant to replace obedience and training.

I remember this prophet training me to hear God's voice one day. He drove three hours to come and train me to hear God's voice. I didn't ask him to do this, but God told him to. It was really remarkable. After I heard the voice of God speak to me like he said, he gave me a huge key. He said earlier in his life he was often being attacked by the devil. He was crying out for God to provide, to heal (I believe in healing more than most anyone I know, so I'm not supporting a theological lack of healing), to deliver him, and more complainant prayers. He said it grew so bad, the devil showed up in his room and threatened his very existence. At that point, a strength rose up inside of him and he shouted, "Take everything, I don't care; Christ is all I need." Bam—the devil disappeared. He said most of the attacks he was incurring were the selfish mindsets he had over serving God.

I truly believe this is the issue. Jesus said this, *"I will no longer talk much with you, for the ruler of this world is coming, and he has nothing in Me." John 14:30 NKJV.* Nothing and nobody of this physical world had Christ's heart. He was so free of this world that He counted those who do His Father's will as His family.[100] The things of this world can have our hearts, and that's all the devil needs to stop us from serving God. It's plain as day; the church as a whole is in love with God providing their needs, but not in love with the God who supplies those needs. We've fallen asleep to the wrong Gospel. If our comfort, our convenience, or friends, jobs, or anything has our hearts in reality, then those

---

100 Matthew 12:50 NKJV

things will daily keep us from following Jesus in the Bible. He's the same today.[101]

All the devil has to do is touch your personal stuff or people to get you away from serving God or to keep us from serving God. The devil only comes to test your profession. Look at Paul, he had hardly anything go right, yet he pressed on to preach the Gospel. When we are persuaded to serve Christ then nothing stops us. If it's truly our heart to do the Father's will, we can follow through. Most of us have breakdowns when we are not celebrated by a loved one, don't get that promotion at a job, lose a loved one, etc., because at some point, there is a belief that God owes me more than He owns me. Are these things hard? Yes, in our present understanding, but this world isn't our reward. Paul said, *"For I consider that the sufferings of this present time are not worthy to be compared with the glory which shall be revealed in us."*[102] What does that mean? This world isn't our reward. His glory and eternity will be. This life is a seed for eternity! It is not a need we need met. The needs-based, entitled, and convenient Gospel has actually allowed the enemy to attack people as a result. It isn't the Gospel in the Bible and it's based on selfish motives. If we as the body of Christ want to overtake the enemy nationally, we must get over our stuff personally. Jesus said, "The gates of Hell will not prevail against us."[103] In that context, it was around the revelation that Jesus was the Christ. If Jesus was the Christ, then we would be following His Way. His Way was to be obedient even to the place of death.[104] That doesn't mean we will die, but we obey even if it means death.

---

101 Hebrews 13:8 NKJV
102 Romans 8:18 NKJV
103 Matthew 16:18 NKJV
104 Philippians 2:5-8

Even if our fears cry out. Even if our spouses disagree. Even if our family thinks we are crazy. Even if society says it's hate. Just like the three Hebrew children said, "We will not bow."[105] Now they believed and stated God would save them, but even if He didn't, they would not disobey. In today's world, we think God would want it easier than it is, but God was never into our ease or comfort; He was into the salvation of this world.

GOD WAS NEVER INTO OUR EASE AND COMFORT AS FAMILIES OR COUNTRIES, HE WAS INTO THE SALVATION OF THIS WORLD.

And they overcame him by the blood of the Lamb and by the word of their testimony, and they did not love their lives to the death. Revelation 12:11 NKJV

In many areas of thinking, the world is ahead of the church. Because of a wrong presentation of the goodness of God, we have interpreted the Gospel to say my way and God has to bless me. God doesn't owe us benefits in this life regardless of what we do. I know Joseph Prince and all the grace teachers have helped legitimately with finding the love and grace of Jesus, but the message of grace wasn't to replace our obedience or training; it was meant to empower it. Look in 1 Corinthians 15:10; Paul worked harder than all the other apostles. Why? Because He knew the grace of Jesus more than anyone. The grace and goodness of God doesn't replace our obedience; they strengthen it.

"And being in anguish, He prayed more earnestly and His sweat was like drops of blood falling to the ground." Luke 22:44 NKJV

---

105 Daniel 3:17-18 NKJV

TRAINING SETS YOU APART FROM OTHERS

I remember hearing a man of God say that if you prayed one hour a day in tongues it would set you apart from other believers. Those who practice get noticed. Those who practice are seen above the crowd. I tell my kids this. I say that the pros weren't originally pros, but the pros are those who practiced the most. They were those who lost their pleasure and practiced what was necessary. Practice sets us apart. 1 Corinthians 9:25 says that Olympians practice a lot to obtain a temporary crown; we, on the other hand, practice for an eternal crown. Why then do we hold back on training? We are so flaky when it comes to God. The world knows that training is the basis of becoming great. Wow, but the church just looks for someone to do it, someone to promote us, someone to give us what God has told us to do it. It's the training that makes us powerful. It's training that trains us for war. It's training that pushes down our flesh so that the Spirit has no argument for future divine appointments. Many people are stuck in their walk with Christ waiting for the next door to open but they are waiting for things that most likely, are waiting on them. Without training, I don't believe we can handle the next promotion or place for which God is preparing us. Look at David; if he had not tackled the lion and the bear, he wouldn't have had confidence in his gift and His God when he came to Goliath.

TRAINING IS THE PROCESS THAT MAKES US ABLE TO HANDLE THE PROMISE.

"The hand of the diligent will rule, but the lazy man will be put to forced labor." Proverbs 12:24 NKJV

"Good planning and hard work lead to prosperity, but hasty short cuts lead to poverty." Proverbs 21:5 NLT

"Therefore if anyone cleanses himself from what is dishonorable, he will be a vessel for honorable use, set apart as holy, useful for the master of the house, ready for every good work." 2 Timothy 2:21 NKJV

It will not happen without it. Whoa, what did you say? Yep, so many believers are just waiting and believing for God to do what He instructed us to do. Hope isn't a strategy to hearing from God or moving with His power on the street. I see this as one of the biggest lies holding believers back. It's demonic because it empowers their flesh. Like God is going to make them a super hero man or woman of God without their obedience to training or discipline. Yeesh, that sounds harsh, but it's the truth! God looks for those who are willing AND obedient.[106] Amen.

"For you have need of endurance, so that after you have done the will of God, you may receive the promise." Hebrews 10:36 NKJV

You cannot give in to failure. You cannot stay down if you fall. Failure isn't a word with Jesus unless you don't start or you just give up. The world we grow up in is based on failure; therefore, I understand the fear here, but let's focus on what I said, "the world." Failure isn't a mentality in the Spirit of God. It isn't a Kingdom mindset, but a worldly one. Even fear that's been medicated as okay in the church world, is just as worldly as smoking weed. What? Yup. Just because it is more accepted and isn't illegal with the law doesn't make it any less worldly. God has called us out of all kinds of darkness, including fear. The world has made

---

106 Isaiah 1:19 NKJV

the victim the hero instead of heroes. That doesn't represent a lack of understanding or compassion, but just a factual reality to what's happening. Most of us have fallen into some alternate reality where we think the Father, Son, and Holy Spirit are on board with our eternal recovery. I'm being a little facetious, but I truly believe that most think fear is okay. It's not; it's a demon that has been accepted in the membership in our churches and that spirit was never qualified. We heal pain, yes, but we don't promote the processes we adopt or lifestyles of fear we honor. Patience yes, but more than patience, we need His power. If we can get honest about our reasons not to move forward, it has more to do with fear of recurrent pain than it does with anything else. Then we can start to be honest with God, "I have these fears Lord, please help me, I'm struggling," instead of making more disciples and generations of timidity or powerlessness.

Failure can be a good thing. Yup, as sons of God, we function under a Spirit of adoption or acceptance.[107] That means our Father really thinks we are awesome. I'm personally won over that He celebrates us trying (walking in faith) but not staying in fear. Think about athletes; they push themselves to failure every day so THAT THEY CAN HAVE NEW GROWTH. It's not different with faith. Faith is a muscle; it's a not panic button to push in times of emergency. So push yourself daily, get out of the box of fear—it's not real anyway. This world and all those who could, should, and didn't accept us was never our reward. Our Father's love fills our need[108] so I can serve Him without the fear of punishment![109]

---

107 Romans 8:15 NKJV
108 Romans 5:5 NKJV
109 1 John 4:18 NKJV

Just think, quitting means giving up everything you've fought for up until now. Don't let your pain be in vain. Let that motivate you against the works of Satan. Quitting has never solved anything. It will just make it easier to quit next time and make you lose respect for yourself. Set a goal and don't give up until you see it.

"For a righteous man falls seven times, and rises again, But the wicked stumble in time of calamity." Proverbs 24:16 NKJV

The fear, and honestly—the loathing—of getting over the hump or fear is the hardest part of following Christ, but comfort isn't our reward. This is why setting goals is so necessary. Thomas Edison took over a thousand tries before inventing the light bulb. You have to say things out loud to yourself like this: *"I give myself permission to make mistakes because that's how I grow."* Goals help us get over the fear of failing.

Some really easy faith daily goals can be the following:

1. Bring a friend along no matter how you practice. This isn't a limitation or a law, but IT'S WAY EASIER. I started mostly on my own but a friend goes such a long way.

2. Don't go home until you see one person healed, prophesied, or had an encounter a day. Getting out there is the biggest thing. Don't condemn yourself if you are too afraid to cross that threshold to talk to a person at the beginning. This is just goal setting, if we don't aim at anything, we usually don't feel led for anything.

3. Pray for two friends or more (there are so many on Facebook) a day until you hear a prophecy drop in your spirit and then message them that word. Just say, I was praying

for you and this came up. Ask, "Does this mean anything to you?"

4. Start to go to prayer meetings at local ministries and push yourself to pray openly if that's allowed. In prayer, you hear from God. When you hear from God, you pray it out loud. This makes His voice a whole lot easier to hear when you are around the public, jobs, friends, and family. If your local ministry doesn't have prayer meetings, start one yourself. When I first was changed by Jesus, I was holding 2 or 3 a week. To this day, I know prayer is the foundation, so we still pray multiple times.

5. Don't leave your job until you have prayed about someone and given them an encouraging word. It's not pressure, but this is training. This is what discipleship looks like. Most likely, ministers won't train you like this, so you have to want this enough to harness yourself.

6. Ask God for details about someone through words of knowledge that will show you who to talk to wherever you are going. This is called treasure hunting. One time when we did this, a lady in the group saw a yellow vest and I saw a yellow big M, but we FELT that it was at Walmart. The local Walmart across the state border had a McDonald's, and there was a guy who was an atheist with a yellow vest right under the big M. God's so fun, and He has the lost—and even believers—in His heart to bring closer to Himself.

7. Watch people who go and do this already. Watch Todd White, Tom Fischer, Pete Cabrera, Torben Sondergaard,

etc., in action. This helps me more than listening to more teaching. It changes the subconscious mentality to seeing yourself doing it. Don't compare, just be inspired. This is the "Jacob process" to success. What you digest is what you expect. So just like Jacob put stripes and spots in front of the sheep to produce more of the same, whatever you put in front of yourself begins to multiply. I've watched hundreds of videos of people doing what I do in order to keep that as the culture of my soul.

8. Start asking God to lead you with discernment and words for people who have an oppression. The enemy cannot touch you if you are truly born again and are filled with the Spirit. Ask them, "Hey, I feel like praying for you— would this be okay?" As you pray, God will give you more specifics. So many people we have prayed for felt "lighter" after we prayed. Some sense tingling, heat, or a cool breeze go through their body. After I pray, I ask if they are sensing anything, just to bring to their attention that something is happening to build their faith. If the oppression or side effects aren't gone, I pray again. I usually pray twice for complete strangers and then tell them I'll pray for them on the way if it doesn't totally break. It just keeps the awkwardness level down. I always offer or ask for their contact information if they want further prayer or to connect later.

9. Take the leap of faith to ask people for prayer and expect God to speak afterwards. Remember, we are growing in this; it's okay if nothing comes. We aren't looking to be pros, we are looking to serve our King. More times than

not, it's after I take the leap to talk to someone or ask to pray for them that a specificity of ailment or issue in their life comes; then I ask them about that. They are still blown away. I mostly say this, "Hey, my name is Greg Gervais. I want to ask you a crazy question." That puts them at ease, because you are recognizing it's already awkward for both of you. Then I ask if there is a pain or regular ailment they have. I do say prayer sometimes, but because that has become a religious word to many folks, I just ask if they want it to go away. Or, if I get a word of knowledge, I still say the same thing, "My name is Greg Gervais. This is a crazy question, but does your right shoulder hurt?" Then explain you are a follower of Christ and He speaks to you about people because He loves them. Remember, they aren't used to professionals coming, they are used to nobody caring!

10. After praying or taking that leap, people are always open for the Gospel, so share it. Jesus died to take away our sins, so we could have a relationship with the Father and be saved from the punishment of our sins! He brought the Way to be connected into a personal and tangible relationship with the Father. This is the best news ever and people need to be saved. It's not primarily for an earthly purpose. You can have an earthly purpose but still not have salvation. Power encounters help bridge the gap to share the Gospel. I have only been rejected twice after a power encounter of prayer with a recipient and I've prayed for about 8,000 people outside the church. They don't need to pray to get saved right after, but if it's open—ask. Ask for a name or number and lead to baptism, yes, with you!

#Every Believer can baptize. You can baptize in a tub and start a movement. Start a house group. It will change your life. You are empowered by the Holy Spirit. Or pray they would be filled with the Holy Spirit right there. Power is with you. Don't quit. Just outlast your feelings and the devil who will try to trigger them. It's a pioneering deal. Just like Isaac had to keep on re-digging the wells of his dad in Genesis 26, we must contend for that. The world depends on us breaking through.

11. Do something. It's better to start to do prayer walks in your neighborhood, the city, Walmart, or even your job than to stay frozen in fear. Start buying people coffee and if they ask why, tell them it's because Jesus loves them. He can change their lives, and then ask if they need prayer for something. You can do acts of service which are a way to open conversations, but at least you are doing something. You are the one to start a new legacy in your life and in your family's life. Jesus needs you!

12. Just take the shot. Overthinking doesn't help anyone; it just shuts us down. Taking the shot is just like James Bond or any trained soldier. They obey first and ask questions later. The only difference is we have a perfect overseer who is in love with the people we are practicing on or reaching out to. It will only be a benefit to your faith and their faith to step out. Fear is the only reason that is holding most of us back, so take the shot.

Lastly, I'll confront one more mindset. People think we can do more wrong trying than not trying. They will say, "Don't we cause more harm when someone isn't healed than if we didn't," or, "What if my word of knowledge or prophecy is wrong? Won't I look like a false prophet,"or, "Isn't training fake or non-authentic?" Although they seem to be legitimate reasons, I beg to differ. The Bible says, "love never fails."[110] The fact that we are out there means we care. Yes, somebody could become a religious zealot but even still, Paul says, "at least Christ is preached."[111] Secondly, training is what Jesus did with the disciples before He ascended. It's training that gets us ready for our calling. Let's shake off all of these arguments that we've accepted and share the Gospel with power as we go. I'm believing for the Holy Spirit to come upon you in a new dimension!

Join me on this journey to open the supernatural for #Every Believer to heal the sick, cast out demons, make disciples, boldly share the Gospel and win the world for Jesus. The largest move of God and the largest army of love, purity, and power is coming together; it is time for us to awaken!

We are equipped by the Word of our Lord and the power of the Holy Spirit to go to war or the war comes to us. What if now is your moment?

#Every Believer can hear from God. #Every Believer can heal the sick. #Every Believer can cast out demons. #Every Believer can live a bold life sharing this great Message. #Every Believer can be anointed to do what Jesus did and commanded us to do. #Every Believer can do what Christ did and commissioned us to do upon His leave. He left us as empowered agents.

We have to be the people and now has to be the moment. I'm praying for the Holy Spirit to awaken a hunger for more, a

110 1 Corinthians 13:8 NKJV
111 Philippians 1:18 NKJV

boldness to cross the line of comfort, and a power to awaken your senses to the anointing He has given to His great army, His people. I pray that as you finish this book, encounters in His presence and glory would begin to fill your life. I pray that His Spirit would follow this book with so many divine appointments with Him all around you. What if you took the leap of faith to move forward? Can you feel the pull? He is waiting.

You can follow my social media platforms for more training, live ministry, and testimonies of what God is doing through #Every Believer.

ABOUT THE AUTHOR

Greg Gervais is a senior pastor, speaker, and revivalist who has a passion to empower #Every Believer to walk like Jesus. He travels nationally and internationally to awaken #Every Believer to the power of the Holy Spirit in them. Greg lives in Southaven, Mississippi, with his wife, Sharrah, and his three kids, David, Elijah, and Abby.

Made in the USA
Columbia, SC
09 February 2023